COMING BACK

The 1993 Chapel of the Air 50-Day Spiritual Adventure
"Survival Skills for Changing Times"

8 Survival Skills for Changing Times, by David Mains. Discover eight practical "life preservers," designed to keep your values and your faith intact in a fast-spinning world. Small group discussion questions and helpful excerpts from other books included with each chapter. Catalog no. 6-3036.

Getting Beyond "How Are You?" by David Mains and Melissa Mains Timberlake. Are you desiring closer connections with others? Do you often feel lonely? Learn the art of moving from small talk to significant and healing conversation. Catalog no. 6-3035.

Coming Back, by Steve and Valerie Bell. Gain inspiration from the stories of spiritual survivors, men and women who found God sufficient in their darkest moments and who offer hope for our own times of heartache and struggle. Catalog no. 6-3037.

Adventural Journals. Dig deeper into the Adventure with day-by-day personal growth exercises. Available in the following editions:

Adult	Catalog no. 6-8820
Youth	Catalog no. 6-8821
Children, grades 3–6	Catalog no. 6-8822
Primary, preschool–grade 2	Catalog no. 6-8823

ALSO AVAILABLE:

Adventure Leader's Manual	Catalog no. 6-8824
Children's Church Curriculum	Catalog no. 6-3101

STEVE & VALERIE BELL

A DIVISION OF SCRIPTURE PRESS PUBLICATIONS INC.
USA CANADA ENGLAND

Unless otherwise noted, all Scripture references are from the *Holy Bible, New International Version®*. Copyright © 1973, 1978, 1984 by International Bible Society. Used by permission of Zondervan Publishing House. All rights reserved. Other references are from *The Living Bible* (TLB), © 1971, Tyndale House Publishers, Wheaton, IL 60189. Used by permission; *The New King James Version* (NKJV). © 1979, 1980, 1982, Thomas Nelson, Inc., Publishers; and *The Authorized (King James) Version* (KJV).

Copyediting: Jerry Yamamoto and Barbara Williams
Cover Design: Scott Rattray

Library of Congress Cataloging-in-Publication Data

Bell, Steve (Steve B.)
Coming back / by Steve & Valerie Bell.
p. cm.
ISBN 1-56476-037-5
1. Christian biography—United States. 2. Trust in God—Christianity. 3. Suffering—Religious aspects—Christianity. I. Bell, Valerie, 1949- . II. Title.
BR1700.2.B46 1993
248.8'6'0922—dc20 92-31419
[B] CIP

1 2 3 4 5 6 7 8 9 10 Printing/Year 96 95 94 93 92

CONTENTS

DEDICATED TO
my wonderful parents
and
Valerie's loving parents-in-law
CLIFFORD AND KATHRYN BELL
in celebration of their
50th Wedding Anniversary
August 30, 1992.

Thank you for my
rich spiritual heritage
and your consistent godly example.

Know you are deeply loved!

PREFACE

Everybody loves a good story. And meaningful stories have tremendous staying power. Storytelling is still one of the most effective teaching methods of all. In fact, who of us cannot recall some significant lessons learned because of the stories we heard during childhood?

Jesus Himself told lots of stories. And His stories (typically packed with emotion) are both appealing and unforgettable. Some of His stories have become so famous (like the Good Samaritan) that even secular society has taken notice.

This book is full of stories. All of them are true; no names have been changed.

When Valerie and I first started this project, I have to confess I had some serious questions about the wisdom of such an undertaking. All of the people you'll meet in this book are personal friends. Some of them are very close, long-time personal friends.

Frankly, both of us were a bit nervous about approaching them with the "opportunity" to divulge honestly regarding themselves because we had this "wonderful idea" that their story—tragedy, spiritual struggles, suffering, doubts, foolishness, sin, anger, frustration with God, lessons learned—could minister powerfully to a lot of other people. To our surprise each one willingly bought in!

We were greatly encouraged . . . for a few hours! For then, our next concern was: "But how honest will they really be when we turn on the tape recorder? What if they kind of candy-coat their experiences and not tell it like it really was?" (And we were close enough to most of these people and situations to know whether or not they were holding back.) Well, again, our concern was unfounded because that did not happen at all. Integrity reigned!

The following pages portray accurate real-life stories of courage from spiritual survivors. These are accounts of God's grace in the midst of intensely difficult circumstances. Our sole purpose in working closely with these friends to put their stories on paper is to minister on behalf of Christ. In no way is this book intended to be an exercise in spiritual voyeurism.

We've designed the format allowing each person to tell his or her own story. And yes, each one has approved all that's been included *before* it went to print.

We believe these stories need to be told. It's our prayer that they will build your faith. And, because of the lessons that can be learned, hopefully, some of these real-life stories will be long remembered.

Steve and Valerie Bell
Summer, 1992

CHAPTER ONE
COMING HOME

Steve and Valerie Bell

Thou hast enlarged me when I was in distress.

Psalm 4:1 (KJV)

The next time you are called to suffer, pay attention. It may be the closest you ever get to God. It could very well be that the hand that extends itself to lead you out of the fog is a pierced one.

Max Lucado
No Wonder They Call Him Savior

God disciplines us by disappointment. Life may have been going on like a torrent, then suddenly down comes a barrier of disappointment; until slowly we learn that the disappointment was his appointment. God hides his treasures in darkness.

Oswald Chambers
The Place of Help

Not everyone who starts with God stays with God. Probably all of us know someone who for a while (maybe even years) appeared to be a solid believer. But then, hard times came—crisis, financial reversal, tragedy—and the person's response was bitterness and disillusionment with God.

Or maybe, that someone is you. Though you still go through the motions—attend worship, give to the church, sing in the choir—down deep, it's all hollow. If that's where you are, we understand.

Life does have its special moments, but also, it can be ruthless. C.S. Lewis put it this way, "Actually it seems to me that one can hardly say anything bad enough or good enough about life." We agree. It's difficult to make sense of it sometimes.

Why is it that one person, who experiences despairing circumstances, is able to survive spiritually, and yet another, facing similar problems (maybe not even as intense), becomes a spiritual casualty? What is it that makes the difference?

Why are some believers able to face the worst life can throw at them, and their faith stays intact—actually deepens—while others seem to fade and fall away?

Why is it that two people can lean over the abyss of faithlessness—one will come back to God, but the other plunges over the edge?

Are there some special secrets to spiritual survival? If so, what are they?

That's what this book is about.

Perhaps right now, you're suspended somewhere between the "survivor" and "casualty" categories. You're not exactly sure where you fit. Since the personal turbulence you're experiencing has not yet calmed down, you're still very much in process and "up in the air" about how your personal story of faith will land.

I (Valerie) can relate. I remember a spiritual crisis over which I nearly lost my own faith.

I was thirty-three. I had just moved back with my family—my husband, Steve, and our two small sons—to my parents' house in Wheaton, Illinois. While sorting through a drawer, I picked up my father's Bible and thumbed through the pages. In flowing handwriting someone had written: "Presented to Wilfred Burton from the Moody Bible Institute Evening Singers on May 23, 1972." I immediately noted that the date was slightly before my father's retirement from that school, where he had served in the music department for thirty-five years.

As I flipped the pages, I noticed with irony that all the entries in the margins were in Mother's compact modest handwriting. Dad never really had a chance to use that Bible. I read Mother's entries, and one in particular stood out: "Apt to think our problems are the worst."

At that moment, once again the distressful images of the past seven and a half years engulfed and overwhelmed me—problems worse than I ever could have imagined! I remembered the phone call early in the morning. "Daddy's sick," they said cautiously, trying not to alarm me. I was twenty-six and was expecting our first baby. What an understatement that proved to be! Daddy had contracted encephalitis (brain fever) and was in a deep, apparently painful coma. Our family filled the following days with fervent, insistent prayers for his restored health and life.

During that initial hospital season, people told us stories of encephalitis survivors. We heard of one woman who had contracted encephalitis while pregnant, recovered, and later delivered a healthy baby! That gave us hope. We waited. He held on.

Eventually the coma lifted. He would survive! We were thrilled!

But then our elation turned to horror. The father we knew had not returned with his body. This "restored" father was alive, but nonresponsive. Encephalitis gave us back a stranger—a man who didn't know us. Encephalitis took our father.

It was a long struggle adjusting to the reality of his condition. What was obvious to the medical community, we could not accept. They tried to tell us gently. But we resisted. We were a family of faith. We believed Daddy would be restored, maybe very slowly, but in time he would come back to us. We prayed in faith, believing, and clung to any sign of response. "Did he seem to recognize an old friend who had come to visit? Was he trying to say one of our names? Did he understand something we had said?"

As the days turned into months, however, and the months dragged into years, we finally had to accept the truth: Daddy's brilliant mind was gone! How strange to realize he didn't know us—would never know us. It was so final, so hopeless. How sad to look into those familiar eyes and see a vacuous stare, or worse, a panicky fearful gape! Our articulate, intelligent father had no more words, and apparently no more thoughts, no memory or ability to learn. He was hopeless, and we were powerless to help.

At his doctors' advice, we placed him in a nursing home. There, among the wandering, pointless, sometimes agitated lives, in a sterile metallic institutional room, permeated throughout with industrial-strength acrid and antiseptic smells, surrounded by lost people clothed in various stages of unbutton and undress, we made Dad's final home.

There were two floors in this nursing home. Dad was on the top floor with the most severe cases. He was one of the worst.

"Oh, God!"

Occasionally he would smile. I remember him responding to the perky, pretty social worker. She was always upbeat. Unthreatening. She talked to him in a Sesame Street voice usually reserved for two-year-olds. It seemed inappropriate to me, in light of the college professor he had been, but Daddy didn't know that. He liked her.

But for me—the sad young mother who, during those years, tenderly brought her newborn babies to him (and he who had been a lover of children was unimpressed and nonresponsive); for me, who held his hand and *tried* to be perky, but never really managed to hide the knot in my throat or the pain in my heart—he never smiled. In fact, it was almost as though I disturbed or bothered him on some deep level. Sometimes he would even push me away. I, who had been his joy, had no power to delight him anymore.

I was nothing to my father throughout his illness. We were all nothing to him . . . nothing to this man who lived only in the present tense, suspended somewhere between heaven and a living hell. Where *was* my father? Only God knew where the real Dick (Wilfred) Burton was—and God wasn't telling.

Silent Fathers.

Distant Fathers.

Powerless Fathers.

In time I stopped pelting heaven with my prayers. I stopped pleading, stopped bargaining, stopped jumping through the spiritual hoops.

Why bother? My Heavenly Father seemed as unresponsive as my earthly father.

As I returned Dad's Bible to the drawer, I sighed, remembering the chain of sorrowful events. In fact, life wasn't getting better. Just six months earlier, in January of 1982—two and a half years after Dad's death—we buried Mom. Throughout the whole ordeal of Dad's illness, Mom had remained tenacious in her faith. In fact, looking back, I realize that during that time, in a sense, she did *my* believing for me. But only two and a half years after Dad's death, we were totally unprepared to lose her. Mom's death was as sudden as Daddy's was slow. It was also full of irony. She died on my sister's birthday. Karen was forty. At the time my brother was thirty, and I was thirty-three.

Worst of all, we had been planning her wedding! She was only six weeks away from being remarried. After enduring those four and a half sad years with Daddy, who was so sick, it was wonderful to see her happy again. We were all excited and crazy and laughing. Finally, a time for celebration had returned to our family. Mom was so alive and in love and telling the world about it! It was as though she had returned to her teen years, completely disregarding her adult children's embarrassment.

And then suddenly she was gone! A massive heart attack—while dancing—and she left us. No good-byes.

We buried her in the beautiful white suit she was planning to be married in.

Six months later my husband and I, with our two boys (Brendan—six and Justin—three), moved from South Florida back to Wheaton into Mom and Dad's empty house. We were supposedly restoring their old place. But what I suspect I was really attempting was an impossible task. In coming home again, I think I was trying to find Mom and Dad—even if it were just the echo of their laughter or the glimpse of a shadow.

But living in their house on President Street only proved one thing to me—they really were gone! There was no residual piece of them left, no friendly haunting. Moving back home had not eased my grief. It had only delayed it. And then, with tears flowing and an overwhelming longing for my parents filling my days, I submitted to the inescapable task of grieving for them.

My physical world, filled with moving-van disarray and the remnants of my parents' household, contributed greatly to my lack of well-being. As I looked around me, the task seemed so massive. I was almost immobilized. I had never been a great "orderer," and this was the biggest mess, the biggest physical challenge I had ever seen.

Our unpacked Bell things competed for space with my parents' leftovers. Boxes of books and magazines, kitchen utensils, family photos, records, old vocal music, and knickknacks built rickety towers toward ceilings. Towels, sheets, blankets, and old clothing spilled unfolded from boxes converting most rooms into cardboard chaos. Worn-out furniture groaned under the weight of packing crates. Trying to be economical, we went ahead and stripped all the rooms of their wallpapers, leaving the entire house in naked anticipation of bright replacements. At first, there was no room in the house that was truly in "livable" condition. Oh, I hoped the place would be beautiful eventually, but initially, it had all the warmth and charm of monastery cells—monastery cells filled with donations from Goodwill!

My outer world perfectly symbolized my inner world—an out of control messy disarray!

I tried to hold on to my belief in God, but everywhere I looked for spiritual comfort and signs of God's presence, I found ill omens instead. Outside my mother's blazing red roses, an anniversary gift from Dad, surrendered to the sad times. As if they knew that my mother was gone, they mourned. They withered on the vine and died and were no more.

I bitterly recalled the entry in my father's Bible: "Apt to think our problems are the worst." The words mocked me. I was angry and offended by such trite spiritual pieties! Seven and a half years of unanswered prayers (from the time when my father first became ill to mid-1982 when we moved back to Wheaton six months after Mother's death) testified against any attempts to bandage my painfully wounded soul.

That was when I began to learn how things truly work in the spiritual world. We do have a spiritual enemy. But it is not God. God is for us. God takes no perverse pleasure in our pain. He feels for us in our adversity. It was primary to my spiritual healing that I clarify the goodness of God's character in my own life.

I became acquainted with my enemy. He is no gentleman. He can be counted on to show up at the scene of our spiritual accidents while our hearts are breaking and the tears are flowing. He knows when we are weak and susceptible to his wooing. Gently he begins his subtle seduction. He comes as a comforter. He courts our souls away from God with consoling phrases like: "You poor thing. No one understands how hard what you're going through is. You deserve your anger and tears. Oh yes, there's that small matter of God. Well, maybe it's time you learned that the only kind of love He gives is tough love—if He even bothers with you at all. He's so holy He probably thinks you deserve this anyway. You really can't trust Him! Just put your little head on my shoulder and feel as badly as you want. Go ahead and cave in—you're much too weak for the problems facing you."

When his perverse seduction is complete, we become angry at God—if we still believe in Him at all. Our problems defeat us, and our fears yank us around.

The mother of a profoundly handicapped child understood the spiritual danger of self-pity. She expressed it in this way: "I looked into the abyss of human sorrow and saw how dangerous and how easy it is to slide into self-pity—to weep over one's fate. I was given the grace to understand that one has to be on guard against such grieving, for it falsifies one's grasp on life and erodes one's inner strength." (From *Power of the Powerless* by Christopher de Vinck, page 86.)

Satan has a powerful tool in self-pity. He's adept at attacking our spiritual strength with lies that stir up feeling sorry for ourselves. His purposes are being fulfilled whenever we buy into thinking "our problems are the worst." He wants to use our pain to make us self-focused, because, when we are, then we won't draw courage from the spiritual survivors all around us. We'll be weakened, instead of strengthened.

As I look back on that seven-and-a-half-year period in my life, I realize that God was ministering to me in a most gentle way. I had picked up a book to read—secular of course. (At that time I couldn't bear anything that smacked of spiritual placebo.) It was called *Pioneer Women* by Joanna L. Stratton. The book compiles true-life accounts of American frontier life from the women who civilized it.

Sitting between piles of books and boxes, escaping my own life, procrastinating in my task of ordering my home, I began reading the following accounts: "The construction of a permanent family home was the first concern of every new homesteader. In the arid parts of Kansas, dugouts and soddies took the place of the more traditional log cabins."

"For many families, simple dugouts carved in the earth were the easiest structure to build. With their shovels in hand, they literally dug their homes into the sides of hills or ravines. Damp and dark year round, it was practically impossible to keep clean, for dirt from the roof and the walls sifted onto everything. And when it rained? One settler wrote, 'the water came through the roof and ran in the door. After the storms, we carried the water out with buckets, then waded around in the mud until it dried up. Then sometimes the bull snakes would get in the roof and fall down on the bed. Mother would grab the hoe and there was something doing until the fight was over!' "

For 302 pages, I read accounts of births that were too often followed by little graves, of prairie fires and locust plagues, of incredible loneliness, untended illnesses, and material deprivation.

With every page, my life was looking increasingly better. My home, full of disorder and needing major attention, had never rained snakes oozing through mud-mucked walls. All the graves in our families were for people near the end of their life spans. There were no little graves bearing our family name.

My problems were not the worst! Others have had much worse problems and survived!

I found the courage of these suffering pioneer women to be contagious. I began to appreciate the little things of life again. I started feeling strangely blessed by the heritage my parents provided me, instead of just grieving their loss. As the weeks passed, and I continued to reflect on the real-life stories of these courageous women, I became increasingly energized for *my* work. I was getting ready to take on my enemy and resist his attempts to turn me into a spiritual wimp.

I began to note the touches of God's grace along the way. I remembered one particularly sweet gift God gave me when my father died. Our family kept a vigil by Dad's deathbed. We read Scripture; we held his hand; we loved him and talked about how wonderful heaven would be for him. He cooperated with his death—though as it turned out it was hard work for him to die. His breathing was labored, as if he were struggling to give birth to his soul. But, though he suffered, he seemed peaceful and accepting of his situation. We made him as comfortable as possible. This time there were no pleading prayers asking the Lord to help him hang on. We had all learned that there were worse things than death. Now we were ready to let him go. We too wanted him released from the prison of his body.

I started to sing at his bedside:

There is a place of quiet rest
Near to the heart of God,
A place where sin cannot molest,
Near to the heart of God.
There is a place of full release
Near to the heart of God,
A place where all is joy and peace,
Near to the heart of God.

Oh Jesus, blest Redeemer
Sent from the heart of God,
Hold us who wait before Thee
Near to the heart of God.

I stopped singing. Then something happened that had not happened in over four years. He looked at me and made a sound as though he was trying to communicate with me. He wanted more singing! For the first time in four and a half years we had connected with each other—and I was able to help him! I then sang, "Softly and tenderly Jesus is calling... come home, come home, ye who are weary, come home...."

He greeted the end of that song with more "uh-uh-uhs." I continued singing—right through the hymnal—each song ending in a command performance for more! I'm sure they heard me all the way down the hospital corridor because I sang full voiced. But I didn't care what anybody thought. Dad had been a voice teacher—my voice teacher, for years. I knew he would want to hear good quality, full resonance, soaring high notes. I gave that to him. It was my last gift—a celebration of his going home to heaven!

But all the music, all the beautiful bitter-sweet music of those days could not hold a candle to the wonderful sound of his gutteral grunt. On his deathbed, he ended his silence toward me. We connected! We connected in time to say, "I love you. Good-bye."

In reality, neither Father of mine—heavenly or earthly—had been as silent as Satan would have had me to believe!

In time, I was restored and came back to a renewed faith. There was no spiritual zap or "evangelical jolt" that got me back on track. It was a process. But I came back—back to God—back to health and spiritual and mental well-being. Life was good again. I would survive spiritually.

However, I came back with a different kind of faith. No longer was it a childish I've-got-all-the-answers, know-it-all faith. Rather it's a childlike faith—simple, trusting, accepting of things I cannot understand or explain, and waiting for heaven where I will no longer " . . . know in part; then I shall know fully."

In time my thinking about God became clear. I began to experience the delight of a faith that declares, "God is *for* me!"

I finally lifted my eyes from myself and looked around me. Others were suffering too. Precious Christian people. I heard their agonizing questions. I saw their pain. And yet, there was a tenacious holding onto God. I've gained tremendous courage from their lives.

In the following pages Steve and I want you to meet some courageous spiritual survivors. These seasoned sufferers have learned important skills for dealing with life's trauma.

Their stories vary. Some have had time to process their grief. Others are coping with a grief so fresh that it's almost impossible to wrap words of meaning around it. Most of the stories are not tied up in nice, neat, little packages with cards that announce: "And everybody lived happily ever after!" For some, closure is still lacking; loose ends remain; and many unanswered questions linger. We've also included stories of people who, in a sense, invited crisis into their own lives. There's all kinds of suffering.

Steve and I offer this book as a gift to all who have struggled spiritually, and we say to you what I sang to my father and myself that day:

> Softly and tenderly Jesus is calling . . .
> Calling, "Oh sinner, come home."

CHAPTER TWO
VISITED BY INNOCENTS

Marshall and Susan Shelley

God has chosen the foolish things of the world to put to shame the wise, and God has chosen the weak things of the world to put to shame the things which are mighty.

1 Corinthians 1:27 (NKJV)

It's hard to express what such a verdict means to a mother. It pierced me to my depth, ripped away the very fabric of life when we discovered how severely different Oliver was going to be all his life. It was not something one could put aside or escape. The world appeared darkened: It was as if the whole of reality had been covered with a grey film.

But over the 35 years (that we had Oliver) I can say there was not a drop of pain left for me in Oliver's reality. He did not change much. He grew to the size of a ten-year-old child. His hands and feet were those of a five-year-old, but he had a thick beard that had to be shaved. He never left his bed. He lay on his back, unable to lift his head, unable to speak, unable to learn anything.

Oliver was always a "hopeless" case, yet he was such a precious gift for our whole family. This child had no apparent usefulness or meaning, and the world would reject him as an unproductive burden. But he was a holy innocent, a child of light. Looking at him I saw the power of the powerless.

I have made my peace with the coming of Oliver's death. I cannot see it as a tragedy. I know that the child who lived in apparent void and darkness sees God, lives forever in health, beauty, and light. Here on earth, he was loved. His presence among us was a mysterious sign of that peace the world cannot give.

Christopher de Vinck, quoting his mother on the meaning of the life of his brother, Oliver, in The Power of the Powerless.

We spent a morning recently with Marshall and Susan Shelley. Marshall, in his upper thirties, works as editor of *Leadership,* a journal published by Christianity Today, Inc. A former college athlete, he now "plays" as coach of his wife's softball and daughter's T-ball teams. Susan, a warm conversationalist, taught public school and directed a Christian day care/preschool center before turning her attention full time to being a mother. Together they take pride and joy in roles as parents of Stacey, Kelsey, Mandy, and Toby. Together they faced a parents' worst fear when two of their four children died within three months.

We were aware that we had asked a hard thing of them. Would they share their fresh grief with us? Time had not had a chance to soften the Shelleys' pain, but neither had it robbed them of their intimate memories—memories they so graciously shared.

Their story is a gift—given through tears. As we sat in the restaurant, we watched Susan talk and cry, and we thought, "This woman is accustomed to tears." We were in a public place, but the tears made a familiar flow down her face until they were dabbed with a gesture of acceptance—a gesture so unheralded it proclaimed, "This is what my life has been like of late. This is normal for a woman in my state."

We wanted to comfort them—to dry her tears. How we hated putting them through the ordeal. We wanted to take them both in our arms and make the pain go away. You will feel the same.

But that is not possible. If we took their tears, we might rob them of the wisdom their pain has brought them. Even they would think that was not a good bargain.

The Shelleys' tears do not indicate weakness. They are a part of their emotional honesty. As they struggle through their story, you will hear their voices—questioning, loyal, tenacious, confused, and angry at times, always articulate . . . but, above all else, they are honest. In that honesty, they have given all spiritual strugglers a great gift. Many will identify with their question: "Where is God?"

Some of the things they said surprised both of us. They also deeply challenged us. We wondered whether we could have handled such sorrow so well. We also felt something that, for lack of a better word, we'll call pride. We have a deep sense of pride in their lives. For though they are honest in sharing their wounds, there is undoubtable evidence that they have survived spiritually. Our sense is that in light of such spiritual tenacity, Mandy and Toby's story has only begun.

Speaking of children like the Shelleys' Mandy and Toby whom you will read about in the pages that follow, Christopher de Vinck has written in a book called *The Power of the Powerless,* "So much depends on how we choose to see things and events. Children like Oliver, Lauren, and Anthony [and Mandy and Toby] exist as is. We decide if they are to be our tragedies or if they are to be our triumphs."

The Shelleys have chosen well.

And so we say, "To life!"—with all its mystery and heartbreak. Here's to those who remind us that living is precious! To Marshall and Susan and Stacey and Kelsey! To Toby and Mandy! To you who take the high hard road, and in so doing give the rest of us hope in our journeys! Thank you! Thank you! Thank you!

❁ ❁ ❁

"We Trusted the Lord"

SUSAN: Well, I guess our story began after the birth of our second child, Kelsey. We love both of our girls very much, but we also wanted a son. As with most couples in America, we had this ideal family in mind, which included both girls and boys. Since our oldest daughter, Stacey, had especially wanted a little brother, we began praying specifically that the Lord would give us a son. We talked about adopting and checked out some possibilities, but that just seemed to be too expensive and too difficult. "Let's have another baby ourselves!" we thought. So we trusted the Lord to give us a third child.

We really hoped and prayed that the Lord would give us a son. At the time I became pregnant, I had strep throat. I was taking medicine, but didn't know I was pregnant. When I found out, I was immediately concerned that the medicine I had taken would affect the baby. At the time I was thirty-six.

My doctor encouraged me to have an amniocentesis done. The test results came back and indicated that we had a healthy female. We should have been rejoicing at the healthy part, but we were devastated at the female part. We went through the next several months disappointed and dumbfounded. We just kept asking, "How hard would it have been for the Lord to make it XY rather than XX?"

The pregnancy went along fine. No problems. Mandy arrived on her due date, which was my mother's birthday—March 14 (1990). It was a very fast delivery, but there was meconium in the birth fluid. So they quickly rushed me from the birthing room to the delivery room.

But the minute the head came out, the neonatologist said, "Let's measure her head; it looks small." Neither of us had any idea what he meant. She looked fine to us. But her head circumference was only 31 centimeters (35 is normal). We heard for the first time the word *microcephaly,* which we later learned means "abnormally small brain." Marshall was there and got to look at the baby, but I really didn't see her for about five more hours. Right after she was born, they took me to the recovery room. Since Marshall's mom was flying in from Denver, he went to pick her up at the airport. So I was left by myself. The doctor and the neonatologist started talking about this child as being microcephalic. I said I didn't know what that was.

"What's Wrong with My Child?"

I do remember the horrible sinking feeling: "What's wrong with my child?" Initially I thought they were talking about dwarfism. I concluded, "Since she's got a small head, that must mean the whole body is small."

Finally they brought Mandy to me that night at about 9. She didn't appear abnormal to me, but I felt such fear as I held her.

The next morning a whole entourage of medical professionals started coming in talking about mental retardation. With microcephaly there was still a 50/50 chance that she could be normal—some children with this condition can even be brilliant; others wind up completely nonfunctional.

We didn't know Mandy's status. Everything else about her body seemed fine. She looked healthy. She had no other anomalies except the small head.

Although we went home from the hospital at the normal time, I was a devastated mother. "My child!" I thought. "There's something wrong with my child!"

I couldn't help but think of all the times we had spent worrying about having a boy—the guilt! Both of us felt ashamed. We should have been praying for a healthy child. Why were we so concerned about the sex? It was just so immaterial.

MARSHALL: Then two weeks after Mandy was born—it was early in the morning—I noticed something kind of strange about her. She stiffened. I was changing her diaper, and her leg started pumping. Just her left leg and not the other. Then I noticed her eyes sort of rolled up into her head. I called Susan. Neither of us knew what was happening.

SUSAN: I'd never seen a seizure before. When they continued, we made an appointment with the pediatrician, then the neurologist, and they started her on anticonvulsive medicine. That was the beginning of her physical difficulties.

At three months we found out she had cataracts. That was devastating because all along I thought she could see me. I thought I was making eye contact with her. Then I realized she couldn't be because her sight, if she had any at all, was like ground glass.

Her cataract surgery was the beginning of a downward spiral. When they pulled out the tubes, all this stuff came out. They discovered she had an infection. She had pneumonia and hepatitis B. She also had strep A at one point—which killed Jim Henson—but she pulled through it all.

Responding in Individual Ways

MARSHALL: By this time, Susan and I were responding to Mandy in very individual ways. Susan took the full emotional ride. I was more inclined to steel myself from feelings. Initially, I thought of Mandy as a project—simply another responsibility. I had to learn to feel real affection. All along, while Susan was seeking eye contact (and assuming there was eye contact!), I guess I felt, "I love this child, of course. I'm going to take care of her. She's defective. I'll do what needs to be done."

Susan's attention, on the other hand, was totally focused on Mandy, the child who needed her most. Meanwhile, I tried to keep some normalcy in life for Stacey and Kelsey.

SUSAN: We had such difficulty getting Mandy's seizures under control. In fact, we never did. She eventually ended up on three different medicines. She was very severe.

MARSHALL: Stacey and Kelsey (ages five and three at the time), also had to deal with all of this. But we never noticed any rivalry. We never noticed any competition. They never reverted to baby behavior to try to get our attention. They never said, "It's not fair!" They never showed any animosity toward Mandy. The only rivalry was who got to hold Mandy first!

SUSAN: In a sense Mandy was like a doll. She didn't do anything other than what their dolls did. They enjoyed cuddling her and that sort of thing. But we did notice that when they played with their dolls, the dolls began having seizures and needing phenobarbital and having to go to Easter Seals for therapy. I guess they just assumed this was normal family life. Sure, babies need medicines. And so they transferred all of that to their dolls.

MARSHALL: We never hid the truth from the girls. We told them from the beginning that Mandy was handicapped. We explained what it meant to be handicapped—that she wasn't going to be normal. We didn't know how long we would have her, but we were going to enjoy her as long as we could. So it just seemed natural that when Kelsey would tell stories about her dolls, she would always have one of them be handicapped. And now she says one of her dolls has died. Since she was almost three when Mandy was born, Kelsey's whole memory is filled with this lifestyle. She's pretty much transferred all that's happened.

SUSAN: Our kids never seemed jealous. Even though there was only so much energy to go around—and Mandy consumed much of it—our kids were really great. You had to know Mandy. She was so unique. She had an ability to draw people to herself. And she always drew the best out of everyone, whether it was the girls, us, the people at church, or medical people. In a strange way, I believe she was really blessed by the Lord. It was as though God totally filled her. There was something that emanated from her—a goodness, a purity. She was so pure! One of the girls said, "You know, Mom, Mandy never sinned." And I said, "You know, you're right. Though she would have if she had been normal. She's not like Jesus. She would have sinned, but she couldn't because of all her health problems."

MARSHALL: Mandy required constant attention because of her seizures. She had to sleep next to Susan at night. We never knew what might happen. Poor Susan would wake if Mandy had even a slight change of breathing pattern.

SUSAN: I didn't sleep well. Mostly I ran on adrenaline. We just didn't know about Mandy. Life was up for grabs. Following the cataract surgery, my hopes were built up that maybe, once the patches were removed, she'd be able to see. Next, they gave her extended wear contact lenses. Then I was so sure she would see me! But, I don't think Mandy ever saw anything. We were pretty certain she was blind. They explained her condition to us in this way: It's as if the camera works, but there isn't any film in it. Because her brain was so severely microcephalic, she couldn't interpret images coming in.

Through that first winter, one problem was that it took forever to feed her. I was able to nurse her for only three months. Since she wasn't gaining weight, we had to bottle feed her. I remember sometimes sitting in a chair for seven hours straight and only getting three ounces down her.

"We Wanted to Hit Bottom"

MARSHALL: And we still hadn't hit bottom. What we were going through was like diving into a swimming pool. We wanted to feel the bottom so we could push off and start figuring out where to go from there. And every time we thought, "Well, seizures . . . that's got to be the worst; then, cataracts . . . it can't get worse than this!" But it just kept up. Every time we thought we had hit the bottom, it disappeared out from under us.

SUSAN: Things kept happening. In February of 1991 (when Mandy was eleven months old), she had to be hospitalized for a week. It was Valentine's Day. She had bronchitis and dehydration. We couldn't get enough liquid into her. They had to teach us how to put a nasal gastric (NG) tube down her nose and throat so that, when we couldn't get her medicine down or enough liquid into her, we could keep her hydrated. Marshall was the one who did that.

All this time Mandy was prone to status epilepticus, which means she'd go into seizures she wasn't able to come out of. When she was just six months old (we had gone back to Denver to visit family) she ended up in intensive care in a Denver hospital. It seemed that everywhere we went she would end up in the hospital. We eventually checked out the hospitals and doctors in Tennessee and Kansas too.

MARSHALL: We started calling these our Club Med vacations!

SUSAN: We were beginning to laugh at how extreme things were.

MARSHALL: Throughout all this, we really appreciated the support of people in the medical field and at church. I knew people always had our best interest at heart. But one of the things that made me angry (in fact, it would make me see red!) was when people approached us and said, "We really don't know how to pray for Mandy. Sometimes we're praying that the Lord would just take her home." And all the time we were working so hard to keep her alive! I knew what they were saying. And in my head I could even see a certain logic to it, but it was a cold logic. Yes, she required monthly trips to the emergency room and enormous amounts of energy, but Mandy was not a burden. Mandy was a gift. We recognized from the beginning that Mandy was a gift. She was a high investment gift, but we recognized she was a gift from God's hand. We were not about to turn around and just give her back and say, "Oh thanks . . . but no thanks!"

"I Was Really Angry"

SUSAN: One person came up to me and said, "The Lord must think you two are just wonderful to entrust you with a child like this. You must be so special to God." I was really angry. I held my tongue, but I wanted to say, "Don't come to me with this. I don't know whether we're special or not, but don't ever tell people such a thing when they're in the midst of their grief. It's a cold, cruel thing to say."

Although some inappropriate things were said, other people were incredibly thoughtful. People who ministered the most were those who simply said, "We're praying for you." Others (of which there were many in our church) would just put their arms around us, give us a hug, and say nothing. There were also people who would cry with me.

Those were the three things that were most helpful: I needed to hear "I'm praying for you!"; I needed to have a shoulder to lean on; and I needed to know that people cared enough to shed a tear—that their hearts were breaking for us too.

MARSHALL: I appreciated those who would express their concern without trying to give any answers. An approach like: "I can't imagine what you're going through, but I'd like to know. Can you tell me?"

SUSAN: Another hard thing, especially for Marshall because

Mandy was so center stage and he felt maybe he was talking too much about her, was when people asked, "How's Mandy?" It was a question that couldn't be answered simply. There was too much to say. Sometimes in one week it was as if we had gone through another whole book with her!

MARSHALL: Immediately when someone would ask, "How's Mandy?" my intensity level went up a notch. Of course, people were genuinely concerned, but if I'd give more than a 30 second answer, for some, that was too much. Most of the time if those who asked weren't close to me, I'd give them a quick response: "We're hanging in there. Thanks for asking." And that usually satisfied them. The people who really wanted to know would get a whole medical update!

"Physical Therapy"

SUSAN: In August of 1990 our doctor encouraged us to get Mandy into physical therapy. So right away we started at Easter Seals. I remember the very first time I walked in, I was almost embarrassed. I thought, "We don't belong here! Mandy's not like these other children." I saw these extremely handicapped children and thought, "This is not my daughter!" I really struggled accepting having a handicapped child.

At this time, we were still hoping her head was growing. It was growing a little bit. But then in September the growth stopped. Meanwhile, I was only going to Easter Seals with Mandy once a week. The way it works, if a child is improving—if the child is showing potential—they'd want the child to go twice a week or more. Mandy never went more than once a week. They really couldn't do any more with her.

I continued to go weekly and joined a support group, which was very helpful. None of the other women were believers, but this gave me plenty of opportunities to share our pain and our hope in the Lord. They were able to share their struggles as well. I was very open with them and open about my faith.

Mandy, however, was the most severe case. In all truthfulness, out of the year and a half that I was in Easter Seals, I never saw anybody more severe than Mandy. But it was also unique, that out of all the children that I saw at Easter Seals,

Mandy looked the most normal. In a sense that was a gift from God.

She was so severe that she never learned to do anything. She was nonresponsive. That was another struggle. As a mother you're set up for your child to achieve. There are all these little milestones—rolling over, smiling, reaching out. Mandy never met one milestone. She never accomplished the most basic action or movement—not even a smile. But I came to the point where I accepted Mandy just the way she was. Though it was a struggle to get to that point. I felt like Jacob at times. I would wrestle with the Lord: "Give us something! Show us some improvement!"

"Real Faith"

MARSHALL: Dealing with all this put a strain on our marriage. The point of tension was over whether or not faith meant to expect God to bring about a change in Mandy. Did faith mean we were to keep expecting God to help Mandy grow and improve and be healed? Or, was real faith accepting her the way she was? I tend to accept whatever God gives me—to me, that's faith.

Susan, however, was very much, "Because I love Mandy, having faith is helping her grow. I'm going to do whatever it takes to help Mandy become all she can be." I was amazed at Susan's persistence. Her perseverance! Her mother's love was going to see Mandy through this no matter what! Every day—stretching exercises to tone Mandy's muscles, making sure she got her medications right on time, feeding her the sufficient amount . . . she had made charts, timetables—Susan was going to do whatever it took to care for this child. That was her act of faith. Being faithful was making Mandy more than she was right then.

I was trying to accept this from God's hand. We were looking at faith from different sides of the coin. Sometimes faith means persistence in asking God to act; sometimes it's accepting what is. At this point in our marriage we came at faith very differently.

SUSAN: By winter (when Mandy was 10 months old), the

doctor told us that she would never walk. But I still think he had hope she would live. She looked so normal. Sometime later the doctor told us her life expectancy would be in the teens, but he seriously doubted she'd get past her twenties. However, he said children like Mandy can die at any time, often overnight. So, we needed to realize that any morning we could walk into Mandy's room, and she might be gone. We were left with the prognosis: Maybe she can make it to her teens, but maybe she'll die tonight!

MARSHALL: That was the other thing that was tough. I always believed we could live through crisis. Things get better or somebody dies, and you take care of it. But this was a continual life-and-death situation. Two years! And somehow in the midst of it all, we had to go to work, brush teeth, comb hair, get kids off to school, teach Sunday School lessons, have birthday parties, call parents, and just sort of do life while our child continues to live or dies.

"The Death of Hope"

SUSAN: I've come to realize that when you have a handicapped child, a child born with a serious problem, right from the very moment you birth the child, in a sense you're bearing the death of that child. It's the death of hope. It's a death of what could have been. The entire time, even though we still had Mandy with us, we were already in the grieving process. We started to grieve at the moment of her birth. She was never going to be this lovely daughter. We were always in and out of emergency rooms. In fact, we became well-known in the medical community. The minute we walked into any hospital, we were greeted by name. We lived very close to death.

Wherever we traveled, Mandy (with all of her problems) came along. When she had to go to the emergency room in Denver or Tennessee—someplace far from home—I was traumatized. But along the way, usually in the midst of great suffering we met so many amazing people. We tried to be faithful. In all these places we had conversations with people about the Lord. In Tennessee and in Denver, in Kansas and in Children's Hospital, at Loyola Hospital, at Central DuPage Hospital—everywhere we went with Mandy, doors opened up for us to talk about the strength that comes from God's people and our hope in the Resurrection.

MARSHALL: Mandy was a conversation piece. No one could hold her for more than a minute and a half without asking, "How do you guys get through this?" And that was an open door to say, "We really couldn't without the Lord, without our church, without our friends." With a child like Mandy we discussed spiritual things naturally because that's what she forced us to think about.

SUSAN: She was one of the most effective evangelists I've ever met! She really was. And we began to feel very privileged to be a part of her entourage.

MARSHALL: She was sort of a celebrity, and we tagged along!

SUSAN: She seemed to point people to the Lord. We just did the groundwork and added encouragement for people to look to God.

MARSHALL: I have to admit that during this time I became somewhat judgmental. Jesus said, "Inasmuch as you did it to one of the least of these My brethren, you did it to Me" (Matt. 25:40, NKJV). I began seeing very clearly what kind of people were drawn to Mandy. Some were unable to look at her. Whether out of fear or some kind of revulsion, I don't know. When she was brought into a room, they'd sort of turn their backs or leave. Yet others watched and quickly asked whether they could hold Mandy. I began to separate the sheep from the goats and think, "If you're drawn to Mandy, you're all right. We're buddies. If you can't accept her, then I can't accept you." Now I know being judgmental like this was wrong, but it was something I struggled with. There were certain people very close to us who were unable to accept Mandy the way she was. I felt like I had been personally rejected because they weren't able to accept my daughter.

"People Loved Her"

SUSAN: But on the whole, people loved her. When there was a church function in the gym or fellowship hall (it almost became a joke!), we'd have to track her down. She'd be in different people's arms and laps. It was amazing! She became the church's child. Many folks remarked about how the church had become so united. People who had been there for years and years—who'd grown up there—said, "I can't remember the church ever being more together and so loving and committed than they were because of Mandy." She was a focal point.

MARSHALL: It was better than a building program! We began to see that maybe there was a purpose in it all. She became our mission, our cause, our conversation piece. She was our ministry. She opened doors for us with people. She became our identity. We were, first and foremost, Mandy's parents. We basked in the glory of being the parents of this very special child. We reveled in that. It seemed like some kind of honor. So many people were drawn to us and became our friends because of Mandy's needs. Certain folks offered to become caregivers and would occasionally keep her overnight so we could get some sleep. This usually happened about once a week. We really bonded with some of these people. So when the Lord took Mandy from us, suddenly our cause, our identity, even some of our newfound friends, were all gone. At least, that's how it felt. Oh, they're still friends, but we don't have the same reason to get together anymore.

SUSAN: Throughout that summer (when Mandy was one year old), it was one emergency after another. Her head had stopped growing at this point. We weren't seeing any positive changes in her. Her seizures were out of control. We had learned how to insert the NG tube down her nose and throat ourselves, but I always had to call Marshall to do that. His staff would go to heroic efforts to track him down at the office!

MARSHALL: Well, that was one of the benefits of being a little more emotionally removed. When it was necessary, I could inflict some pain on Mandy because it was for her own good. Susan was so emotionally bonded that the thought of forcing something down Mandy's nose was unbearable.

"A Note Like This"

SUSAN: Then, in March 1991, we began wondering about the possibility of having another child. Did we dare even consider such a thing in light of all of Mandy's needs? But could we end on a note like this? What we were experiencing was like going to a beautiful symphony, but having the last note of the concert end in a discord. There was still a longing. We thought that perhaps having a normal child would help us carry on. We were only in the discussion stage when, to our surprise, we found I was pregnant again. We were worried.

MARSHALL: The thought of caring for another child on top of what we were already dealing with was hard to imagine.

SUSAN: It took us a couple of months to adjust to the idea. I spent a lot of time crying, just trying to figure out how I was going to manage this.

MARSHALL: At this point there was no boy versus girl issue. We were just praying for a healthy baby.

SUSAN: We already had three girls, so we figured this would be a girl anyway. In fact, we'd gotten the video of *Little Women.* Our two older girls really enjoyed watching it. We thought our home would be like that movie. In that family were four girls—one with a handicap.

I remember the girls asking, "But Mommy, what if this baby is handicapped too?" I remember saying, "We're going to love it anyway. We love Mandy, and we're going to love this one however it turns out." But, in my heart, I was sure this baby was fine. God just wouldn't allow this to happen two times in a row. When people found out I was pregnant, they'd walk up to us after church and say, "We're praying for you every day—for the health of this new child."

MARSHALL: In my mind I responded, "I'll wait and see and assume no conclusions before the book ends."

"I Was So Excited"

SUSAN: People would say, "This is going to be the healing that you need for your family." Meanwhile, the doctor had asked me (I was thirty-seven at the time), "Do you want an amniocentesis?" I said, "No, we had one done with Mandy, and the results came back that she was a normal female, and look at her! Besides, discovering an abnormality wouldn't change a thing. What would we do anyway?" So we didn't schedule the test.

But at about twenty weeks—halfway through the pregnancy—I decided I would like to have an ultrasound test. There was a part of me wanting to make sure the baby's head was the right size and developing properly.

So I went for my ultrasound, and the doctor asked, "Do you want to know what sex the baby is?" I said, "No, I really don't care. We're pretty sure it's going to be another girl." She immediately said, "No, it's a boy!"

I thought, "I'm not going to tell Marshall. I'll keep this all to myself and surprise him." As I left the clinic, they assured me they'd call and let me know the results of the ultrasound as soon as possible.

For the next two weeks, every night I looked at baby books, thinking about names, wanting to find a name that means God hears or God answers. I kept thinking, "Isn't God fantastic? All these years we've prayed for a son, and we got three daughters. And the last daughter's such a challenge. Now finally, God's giving us a boy!" I just couldn't believe it!

I was to go back to my doctor in two weeks, and in the meantime my friends kept asking whether I had received the results of the ultrasound. I said, "No, they'll probably tell me when I return for my appointment."

As soon as I arrived for the scheduled appointment, my doctor asked me to sit down. She said, "I couldn't do this over the phone. We've got problems."

I thought, "It's another Mandy!" I asked, "What kind of problems?"

"Well, the head's small. In fact, the baby is small all over. I'm not exactly sure. We need you to go immediately to Rush/St. Luke's Hospital in Chicago for an extensive ultrasound to find out what's wrong."

I went home and told Marshall. We wondered whether this was genetic. We tried to be hopeful: "If it's microcephaly again, at least there's a wide range of conditions. Maybe this baby won't be as severe as Mandy." Two days later we went to the specialist.

MARSHALL: We thought the worst we could possibly hear was that we had another microcephalic child.

But the specialist explained that this child had multiple birth defects: The cerebellum of the brain was mostly missing, or it was very small. He also thought the baby had cleft palate. And he was sure his heart was assymetrical with the aorta attached incorrectly, and the child had a club foot. "There might be other problems, but these are the ones I can see," he said. He suspected it was a chromosomal problem called Trisomy 13. It was a condition "incompatible with life." He recommended we terminate the pregnancy.

"Stunned"

SUSAN: He was so matter of fact—so unfeeling. We were stunned. We learned that these babies can live up to a month, or a couple of months at the most. Most of them die in the womb—just miscarry. But we told the doctor, "No. God is the giver of life. God is the taker of life. That's not our role or our decision."

MARSHALL: I remember the specialist asking Susan, "Do you want to carry this baby to term?" Susan responded very clearly, "Yes, I do. This child has only nine months to live, and all of them in my womb. We're going to make these months the safest and most secure possible for this baby. If that's the only time I have with my child, I don't want to shorten it."

SUSAN: It was our child—our son—the boy we prayed for for so long. I wanted to know him in whatever limited way possible. Unfortunately, he didn't move much. He was a calm little child, and his condition kept me from feeling him.

MARSHALL: There was something heroic about what Susan did. I don't think you can force anybody to be this way. You can try to inspire people to be heroic—but to be a hero or heroine—one has to volunteer for that job.

I was just amazed at Susan at this point. With sorrow coming our way again, our choices were either to flee from the sorrow, to wipe it away as quickly as possible; or, to lean into it—to accept the sorrow even though it meant more months of grief. We decided to accept it and to look for meaning in this relationship with our son—even though we couldn't hold him apart from the womb.

SUSAN: However, I have to be honest. When we found out how bad the baby was I felt betrayed. I was totally embarrassed. I had made such a fool of myself.

MARSHALL: At that time I thought it was so naive to believe that God was a bearer of good gifts. And to think that we actually thought He wanted to bless us! Ha!

SUSAN: Marshall received the news of the baby's condition and the news that it was our longed-for son all at the same time. I felt like I had been stabbed in the back. I remember conversations I had with God. I asked, "What were You doing during those two weeks? Were You laughing at me while I was praising You? I was rejoicing in You—because You had given us a boy-child! But what's going on?"

I feel differently about it now. I'm sure God was grieving with us. I'm convinced He hurt with us. But at the time it was like, "What a fool I've been to trust Him!"

"Life Had Seemed Good Again"

MARSHALL: Life is so ironic. Before we learned this bad news, life had finally seemed good again. We had been very affectionate with each other. Susan was so warm and loving. The romance in our marriage was better than ever. Life just seemed so good!

But when the doctor spoke that phrase to us, "Incompatible with life," everything changed.

SUSAN: We named our baby Toby. His name means "God is good"—a statement of our convictions, though we had a hard time feeling that way then. The medical predictions were that he would not survive in the womb through that summer. However, though he was so tiny, he hung on.

And, of course, all this time we're still dealing with Mandy's problems. What a horrendous summer that was! Mandy's condition worsened, and she ended up in intensive care with pneumonia. At three different times she went to the hospital with pneumonia. There were a couple more hospitalizations after that. The last one was in August. She was throwing up. We took her in on a Monday night, and they didn't bother putting her on antibiotics this time. They felt it was just a little flu bug. She was given an IV to provide liquids and nutrients. By Wednesday morning our doctor said, "She looks great. I think she'll go home tomorrow or maybe even tonight." But that night she slipped into a coma. Nobody understood what had happened. They tracked me down the next morning. "Get in here immediately. Things are really bad!"

MARSHALL: I rushed from work to the hospital. The doctors didn't think she would make it through the afternoon. All her vital signs were deteriorating.

SUSAN: Her heart rate was slowing down. Her respiration was down.

MARSHALL: Her temperature was 97 . . . 96 . . . 95.

SUSAN: She was puffy. She was white. They told us those were signs of death. Anyway, we kept a vigil, and people from church spread the word through the grapevine. People came and sat with us—prayed with us for her. She made it into the evening. She still hung on. I stayed the night and couldn't sleep. The alarms on the machines kept going off. It looked like we were going to lose her. There I sat, knowing that Toby (the child in my womb) was going to die at birth. I struggled with the Lord. I told Him, "You can't do this. You can't take Mandy on top of the loss of our baby boy! I can't handle losing both of them right now."

MARSHALL: Our pastor, Gary Gulbranson, was there. Susan told him, "The Bible says that God will not give us more than we can bear. Right now I can't bear to lose Mandy knowing that in another couple of months we're going to lose our son. God just can't do that!" And Gary prayed to that end. Susan stayed up all night, praying that prayer.

"It Was a Miracle"

SUSAN: The next morning at 7, the nurses were in Mandy's room, and all of a sudden she opened her eyes. Her heart rate, temperature, and respiration returned to normal, and the next day she went home! It was a miracle!

Later, we found out there were several other people who stayed up that night praying for Mandy. It's the first time in my life I've ever seen such a desperate prayer answered. We've always heard that prayer changes things. But I had never personally seen a live example of people's prayers really changing something. Without question, prayer had changed the events of that night. God heard my desperate plea and gave us Mandy back. I believe He relented. I have no doubt about that.

MARSHALL: Three months from the time Mandy came back to us, Toby was born. He was in distress in the womb, and they asked whether we wanted him to be delivered alive. We said, "Yes!" But he was going so quickly. They delivered him in time to put him on Susan's chest. We held him. We tried to make sure that he felt our touch, felt our breath, knew our voice . . . and then, very quickly he left us. He lived only two minutes.

SUSAN: Toby was six days short of term. He was born on November 22, 1991.

MARSHALL: They always say, when a child is born, it's a miracle. But, when a child is born and dies within two minutes, it's as if eternity has just intersected earth. Birth, life, and death in such a short span of time. It was a holy moment. I remember holding Toby's body just moments after he stopped breathing. My dad was there. He put his arm around me, and we just wept together. Even as that was happening, I thought, "This is probably the saddest, the darkest moment of my life to this point." But there was also something sacred about it. It was a moment when God was there in the grief. It wasn't a happy occasion at all. But we just knew that there was more going on in those moments than we could see. More than we could touch. More than we could feel. There was another presence. It almost requires mystical language to try to explain.

In the months that followed, different parts of Scripture really came alive to me. But other parts seemed almost unbelievable. I'd kind of choke on the words. All those verses about "Whatsoever you ask in My name . . . Is anything too hard for God? . . . Call unto Me and I will answer thee . . . " I just couldn't relate to those passages at all.

And yet other Scriptures stood out in technicolor, like Job 23 or the Book of Habakkuk. Habakkuk complained to God about His apparent injustice. And God responded by describing His mysterious and severe ways—plagues, pestilence, judgments. But God says, in essence, "I won't explain Myself, but I'll show you My glory," which will cover the earth "as the waters cover the sea" (Hab. 2:14). We realized, as Habakkuk did, that "The Lord is in His holy temple; let all the earth be silent before Him" (v. 20). We too had run out of words to say to God, but we stood in His awful and awesome presence. These kind of truths ministered to me.

"They've Encouraged Me"

SUSAN: You would be amazed at all the things that happened through Mandy's life. One time Marshall had gone to the chapel at Children's Hospital to pray while Mandy was having her cataract surgery. In those moments he had written a little prayer for Mandy and left it in the notebook there for parents to write in. Months later, somebody gave us the "Willow Creek" magazine in which a woman wrote about her daughter's heart surgery at Children's Hospital. The mother wrote of her fears and anxiety for her child. At the end of the article she mentioned going to the chapel and finding a prayer that spoke to her. It was Marshall's prayer for Mandy. The woman wrote, "I don't know these people—Mandy, Marshall, and Susan—but they've encouraged me." We were stunned! Our struggle, expressed only to God, had given courage to someone else!

MARSHALL: Through all of this our question was not so much, "Why is this happening *to us?*" We both know Christians who have gone through tremendous suffering. Believers are not immune. But our question was more, "Where is God in this?" He just seemed so absent. And yet, when Mandy went in for her cataract surgery, it suddenly dawned on me, God had led us to a Christian doctor, Jim Judge, who had put us in touch with a Christian pediatric neurologist. He's the one who asked us, "Where are you leaning for support these days?" We said, "The Lord and the church." That's how we found out he too was a believer. One of the residents who was doing the surgery on Mandy's eyes talked to us and said, "I want you to know that I'm a believer and I'm praying for you." The woman who fitted Mandy's eyes for contacts said, "Are you believers? I heard from one of the residents here that you are. I just wanted to let you know that I'm a believer too and I'm praying for you."

SUSAN: We counted in those first three months of Mandy's life, seven different key Christian people in the medical community who came into contact with us to help Mandy.

MARSHALL: It was sort of like "I spy! I spy God!" We suddenly realized we couldn't say, "Where's God?" anymore. God was there in His people—the seven Christians in various medical offices—they were "God in a body" to us. We began to look for God's presence in the people who came our way. If there ever was a time when the church "got it right," this was it. At our church, Glen Ellyn (Illinois) Bible Church, people continually offered such creative means of support. We felt indebted to everybody because of what they were doing and how deeply they cared.

It seems like the church in America is always getting dumped on. But in our case the church was wonderful! I'm proud of the way people responded. And the maturity of the comments! Most would put an arm around us and say, "We can't fathom what you're going through, but we want to do something. We want to pray for you." Then others would share a grief they too had suffered. Some would come and say, "I too lost a child. He was two years old." We came to realize these were special gifts—gifts that came through the sharing of pain.

SUSAN: They also stood with us when Mandy died. It was February 27, 1992. From the time Mandy "came back" to us from the coma she had been relatively healthy. But in October, we had to put a feeding tube into her stomach to feed her. Then in December we found out she had acute glaucoma—yet, as far as a fever or flu—none! In mid-February she suddenly came down with pneumonia.

She was coughing in fits. Since it really scared us, we took her to the emergency room in the middle of the night. She started doing better within a few hours, and we thought we'd be able to take her back home, but we couldn't get her off the oxygen. So she remained in the hospital.

On Sunday morning, since our children's choir which I direct, was singing in both services, I asked Marshall to call the hospital before I left. I had awakened that morning with an uneasy feeling. It was like something was grabbing at my heart. Sure enough, when Marshall called, we learned that Mandy had gotten a fever during the night.

Sunday afternoon they did another X-ray. What had been a little pneumonia on her right side and a little on the left now looked like someone had splattered her with a snowball. I still hoped that God would come through. I thought, "Mandy's Mandy. She'll just surprise us all!"

The next few days were touch and go. On Thursday she went into a bad seizure. She was moaning terribly. Her kidneys shut down. She wasn't urinating. She was so bloated. That afternoon she slipped into a coma. Whenever we'd move her, just from arm to arm, she would moan.

"A Tremendous Impact on People's Lives"

MARSHALL: Mandy continued to have a tremendous impact on people's lives—even while she was dying. One afternoon a social worker dropped by and asked, "May I come in and sit with you for a while?" It was apparent she wanted to say something. She started talking about her divorce . . . a bad second marriage . . . how she was estranged from God but wanted to get back to Him. We talked about that for quite awhile. Obviously she needed to express to someone her desire to get back in touch with God. She was just one of the people who was drawn to us because of Mandy and our suffering.

SUSAN: That Thursday evening we had gone to the hospital cafeteria to eat when they came to get us. We hadn't been out of the room for more than five minutes when Mandy went into a seizure and died. We rushed to Mandy's bedside, and they were still doing CPR. They continued for five more minutes. She was gone.

MARSHALL: Three months from the time when we prayed for an extension of Mandy's life, Toby was born. Three months after Toby's birth and death, Mandy went home to the Lord. Yes, we lost her—but we really do feel that the Lord gave her to us an extra six months!

SUSAN: We did a balloon launch at the burials for both Toby and Mandy, releasing balloons to symbolize our releasing the children to the Lord. We'd prepared a white balloon for Mandy. When we got the graveside, the director said, "I'm sorry. I was holding all of the balloons, but the white one got away. We're getting another one though." His associate hurried to get another.

When we had the actual launch, we let Mandy's white balloon go first. It went virtually straight up. The others, all pink ones representing the rest of us, went up diagonally and horizontally. I don't know how it happened meterologically, but Mandy's continued to go straight up.

Both these events—the balloon escaping the funeral director's grasp and then ascending more rapidly than the others—were like a symbolic message from the Lord. Mandy wanted her spirit to go. She was ready to go even before Toby was born, but we weren't ready to let her go. God was merciful and allowed us to keep her a little longer. But she was so eager. Her spirit was eager. That balloon went straight up!

❁ ❁ ❁

"Through the Eyes of Parents Who Loved Her"

What a gift it is to see a child like Mandy through the eyes of parents who loved her! The Shelleys would say that children like Mandy are undeniably physically and mentally handicapped, but that they are also spiritually gifted. We would agree. The Mandys of this world challenge us to look beyond the obvious disappointments and limits of her life to the impact she had on all around her. Like tiny fleshly icons, these children raise our eyes to God. They have the power to make us ask hard questions we might otherwise avoid. We ask, "Why?" We ask questions about the meaning and value of life. These children force us to face the God-issues we try so hard to shove beneath the surface of our daily lives.

One look at Mandy, and our lesser disappointments—the sex of our children, or the intelligence of our children, or the beauty of our children—take on a clearer perspective. We agree with Marshall and Susan: There is power in a life lived out almost entirely on a spiritual plane. We may be attracted to her or repulsed by her, but no one can ignore a child like Mandy. For those of us who allow her to enter our lives, we may come to understand that the meaning of Mandy's existence has implications for our "normal" lives as well.

We've been deeply moved by the heroism of Susan and Marshall. In a society that's deteriorated to the point that parents are demanding the elimination of their unborn children of inconvenience, the Shelleys' love for Mandy stands in marked contrast. It's impossible to deny the toll Mandy's living took on the Shelleys; yet they express a sense of wonder with her life that downplays the day-to-day burden and bother. They fought to sustain her life—a life so needy that it defined almost all aspects of their daily existence. There is no question that they grieve her loss. There is no sense of relief in her passing. If possible, we're certain they'd have her back—just the way she was.

There's a mystery here that those of us who haven't loved and cared for an extremely needy child like Mandy struggle to piece together. We may not understand it; but the love, acceptance, and yes . . . celebration of this child are there for us to behold.

When we initially approached the Shelleys about sharing their story with us, Marshall said something very interesting: "This is one time the church really got it right!"

When we, members of the body of Christ "get it right," we are an enormous absorber of one another's pain. In reality, the church is a community of suffering. By design we're to share one another's grief and to carry one another's burdens. We are sympathetic by choice, not simply by similarity of experience. We choose to enter into one another's brokenness. We choose to cry with one another. We choose to participate in one another's disappointments and suffering. We choose to identify with one another's losses and grief. When the church operates as a community of suffering, she is incredibly beautiful. There is no organization on the face of the earth like the church!

Mandy was the "church child." A lot of churches have them. In fact, within the church they often have "celebrity" status. They are highly valued. Watch them being carried or wheeled by many different hands every week. Listen to how they are cheerfully greeted and welcomed. Often they are absorbed into the body in a very special way.

Picturing the Shelleys trying to find Mandy at the end of a fellowship time at church . . . hearing how certain church members regularly volunteered to stay up at night with her so the Shelleys could get some much needed rest . . . learning of their pastor, Gary Gulbranson, praying that desperate prayer, "Father, please don't take Mandy right now because it's more than Susan can bear" . . . all of this makes us extremely proud to be a part of this caring, loving, sometimes crying, body of Christ.

The church, though admittedly imperfect, has always stood in sharp contrast to the world around it. Back in the third century a man named Cyprian wrote a letter to a friend, telling him of his decision to convert to Christianity. Here's how he described it:

> This seems a cheerful world, Donatus, when I view it from this fair garden, under the shadow of these vines. But if I climb some great mountain and look out over the wide lands, you know very well what I would see. Brigands on the high rocks, pirates on the sea, in the amphitheaters men murdered to please applauding crowds. It is a sick world, Donatus, an incredibly sick world. Yet, in the midst of it, I have found a quiet and holy people. They have discovered a joy which is a thousand times better than any pleasure of this sinful world. They are despised and persecuted, but they care not. They have overcome the world. These people, Donatus, are the Christians, and I am one of them.

We feel the same pride when we think about "church babies" and the church as a community of suffering. To the secular press and other critical observers of religious life, we say "THESE people . . . (oh ye church critics pay heed!) THESE people are the Christians, and we are among them."

Appropriately, we want Marshall and Susan to have the final word in the telling of their story:

What Mandy Means to Us

Mandy's name means "worthy of love," and when we bestowed that name on her, we had no idea how prophetic it would be.

From the moment she entered the world, she was unlike most children. She never indicated she could see or hear. She never reached out her hand to grasp. She never made a demand or even a request.

She didn't even own anything. Just some medicines, some clothes, and a stuffed animal or two. But her life gave testimony to the truth that life is about LOVE not possessions.

And in love, she was rich. She seemed to attract it from amazingly diverse people. But more amazingly, for one who couldn't walk or talk, she seemed to give love to those she loved.

Truly, Mandy was a gift from the Lord.

CHAPTER THREE

ILLEGITIMATE AFFECTIONS

Ed Sansovini

Though I have fallen, I will rise. Though I sit in darkness, the Lord will be my light.

Micah 7:8

There is no pillow so soft as a clear conscience.

French Proverb

Sin that's been confessed, wrestled with, and overcome is one of the finest teachers we have. Our struggles and defeats can increase our spiritual growth just as much as our victories—if we learn from them.

David Swartz

Dancing with Broken Bones

"Show me a hero," wrote F. Scott Fitzgerald, "and I will show you a tragedy." Intrinsic to the concept of *hero* is the idea of struggle—struggle that is faced more bravely and resolved more triumphantly than by the average man.

Perhaps that is why George Gallup reports that 70 percent of Americans state they have no heroes in *The Day America Told the Truth.*

This national dilemma is understandable. It's hard to look at the super athletes, screen idols, or political figures offered up for public adoration and feel anything that makes our hearts want to beat to the word *hero.* Such persons seem simply to be the combined products of fortunate genetics and a billion dollar image-making industry. Indeed, the people who strive to be our American heroes are better suited for selling gym shoes than inspiring courageous living. No wonder 70 percent of us refuse to be impressed with them. It's getting harder to believe in heroes these days.

Where are the heroics? Where's the pathos? Where's the swimming against the stream? Where's the sacrifice of self for a greater ideal? Where's the courage that challenges us to look inside and measure our own character?

We've always found our heroes while sitting in church pews. As children in the church, the Bible characters were our heroes: Noah, Abraham, Moses, David, Solomon, Samson, Daniel, Esther, Elijah, the Marys, Martha, Peter, Paul . . . to us, their names evoke so much! They've always been so human—sinning and sinned against, angry and afraid, yanked around by their emotions, asking the hard questions like "Why?" and "Where are You, God, now that I need You?" falling and rising again, bent under God's discipline and buoyed up by His love, reduced to simple trust and dependence on God. These personalities from the pages of Scripture were often broken heroes; but through it all, they displayed a tenacious loyalty to God. They were God's champions.

We're still finding our heroes in church pews. Perhaps Madison Avenue would find them unmarketable, but the broken heroes that so characterize the body of Christ do move us. In our thinking, Ed Sansovini is one of them.

Ed is not an average American. Neither is he your average American hero. He's a broken hero.

We first met Ed and his family back in the mid-'70s. I (Steve) was a young pastor in South Florida, and the Sansovini's son, Rick, was a part of our youth ministry. The Sansovini family was always very gracious and supportive toward Valerie and me—especially Ed. In fact, he often made an extra effort to look out for us. He took an interest in our lives, and along the way, provided a few special perks to a financially limited ministerial couple.

Some will look at Ed's life and see a great tragedy. Others will see a tremendous struggle over which he eventually prevailed. Undoubtedly, some have thought him foolish to have allowed an old-fashioned concept like sin to yank him around. And yet others will recognize a man for whom guarding self-respect was primary.

We see someone who made a terrible mistake. We see a man who sinned, but who also, in the face of great humiliation and embarrassment, humbled himself and chose the right, painful, courageous solution—hardly the easy way out. We see someone for whom self-respect and having things right with God were more important than any public image.

We see a man who has been bent by God's discipline and has come through the experience amazed by God's love. His story champions God. He's a tenacious believer—a modern day church pew hero. We're proud to introduce you to Ed Sansovini. May each of us learn from his honest vulnerability in the following pages.

❀ ❀ ❀

"On Top of My World"

I was on top of my world! I had won sixty-six different awards in my industry. I was named "International Marketing Executive of the Year." I served as international president of the Hotel Sales and Marketing Association, and I had been inducted into two halls of fame in our industry. On numerous occasions I was invited to be a guest lecturer at prestigious universities like Cornell, Penn State, Michigan State, and

Washington State. I had reached what I felt was the pinnacle of my profession. I had even been invited to the White House! All of my career goals had been accomplished, and I sensed the Lord's blessing on my life in every way. Life was wonderful. I had been successful and was looking forward to retirement within a few short years. Everything seemed to be set. But there's that verse in 1 Peter 5:8 where we're warned: "Your adversary the devil prowls around like a roaring lion looking for whom he may devour."

I thought I was living for the Lord. I had regular devotions. In my mind, I was untouchable—happily married for thirty-eight years. In fact, within my industry they called me "Iron Horse," because I wouldn't budge on my convictions or give in to temptations that came along. I was in the luxury hotel business and didn't even drink. Nor did I participate in any of the other "questionables" that confronted me regularly on the job. I was a committed Christian, and I made it known. "Iron-minded Sansovini . . . squeaky clean"—that's how my colleagues referred to me for nearly forty years.

But I became distracted, and in a period of weakness, I went off track spiritually. I developed what I call an "illegitimate affection." Before I realized it, I fell into sin. I was in serious trouble. The devil was looking for an opportunity to involve me in something illegitimate. And he won out.

The Bible says, "Set your affection on things above, not on things on the earth." For a time, I focused on the temporal. I was living high, and money came easy. I always carried several one hundred dollar bills in my pocket. That was no big deal.

For fourteen years I had been an executive officer at a large five-star, five-diamond resort hotel on South Florida's Gold Coast. In fact, the owners of this 300 million dollar facility had been so pleased with my performance that they gave me a lifetime contract—something almost unheard of in this business. In early 1984, however, I stumbled upon a scam (evidence of kickbacks) taking place within the organization. It involved several hundred thousand dollars and fifteen people, not all employees. I told these men what they were doing was wrong and that I was going to turn them in.

But following through on what I knew I should do was very hard. These were my friends, my business associates. I had known some of these people and their families for years. One for forty years! While still in a quandary over all of this, I was given a plain white envelope with fifteen one hundred dollar bills inside. When it was handed to me, I was advised just to keep quiet, and there would be lots more "envelopes" to follow.

"That's Not Your Money"

From the moment I kept that first envelope, I realized it was wrong though I never spent a dime of it. This may seem strange, but I put the money aside in a special fund, knowing that someday I was going to have to give it all back. I just kept thinking, "Sansovini, that's not your money." Whenever I thought about putting a stop to it and trying to reconcile the situation, I experienced this huge internal struggle. It all seemed so complicated. So I'd just give in to the enemy and the temptation, and I allowed the scam to continue. The total amount of money I received (over a two-and-a-half-year period) added up to about $130,000. I didn't conceive the idea, nor did I orchestrate it, but I did get involved. This went on during 1984, 1985, and 1986.

In the year that followed—I guess the easiest way to explain it is—I became a wreck! I had always been an extrovert. I enjoyed life, was socially active, loved to be with people. But my whole personality changed. I turned into an introvert. My health started deteriorating. I was gaining a lot of weight. My wife, Jeanne, had no idea what I was involved in. But she knew something was wrong. She repeatedly said, "You'd better go see a doctor!"

I didn't even want to go to church anymore. I didn't want to have devotions. I felt like I was the worst person in the world.

I became desperate for help. I had to share the truth with someone. So I confessed it first to the Lord. Scripture tells us (as David said in the Psalms), "Against Thee only have I sinned." I confessed my sin and claimed 1 John 1:9. Then I went to see a Christian psychiatrist hoping that he could help me further. I told him everything. But he didn't know what to do. I saw my family doctor who's a Christian, and it was obvious to him my problems were much deeper than just physical. I went to my pastor, who's a wonderful person, and he listened to the whole story and then prayed with me. I was trying to follow the biblical steps, and my pastor was very supportive. He cared deeply, but he could only be of help to a certain point. I was the one in the mess, and I'd have to be the one to untangle it.

So I started going to attorneys. I wanted to turn myself in, but needed legal assistance to know how to go about it. In the eighteen months that followed, I went to four different lawyers, spent several thousand dollars trying to find help, but got nowhere. I even told the others who were involved in the crime with me that I was planning to go to authorities and turn myself in. (I knew they would find out sooner or later, so I might as well let them know in advance. In response, one man actually threatened my life.)

I was up front with each attorney. Most of them knew who I was because I was a leader in our industry with a high profile in the community. I had been very active in civic and religious circles in our area. I told them that I had committed a crime and wanted to correct it. I explained exactly what I did—and all four of the attorneys, one by one, said to forget about it. I was told, "You're not accused of anything. Why turn yourself in? You'll get yourself in a lot of trouble. You're just going to open up a can of worms. There are other people involved. Why implicate them? Why create more problems? Just let it go. You'll never get caught."

I was very surprised at their advice. But the worst part was, it wasn't helping me at all. I told them I was a Christian. I told them I couldn't sleep at night. I explained how I felt—that I had violated my values, my credibility, and I just couldn't keep on living with this hanging over me. I asked, "What about my conscience? What do I do with all the money that's illegally in my possession?" I didn't want it! They encouraged me to give it away—perhaps to a charity. I said, "But that's no solution. I've *got* to correct this! The Bible's very clear about believers having to make things right. Whatever the consequences, I'm willing to accept them." The response from each of these attorneys was: "There's nothing I can do. My advice is that you forget about it and move on with your life."

With each passing month I only felt worse. I was increasingly desperate. I gained more weight. I became very depressed. I was having terrible headaches. My body felt my guilt. I was under such intense conviction that I'd look around at our congregation of 2,000 during church services convinced that I was the worst sinner in the crowd—often I'd start to cry. I'd sit in a restaurant and for no apparent reason begin to cry. I'd be driving along in my car, and I'd be crying. I would close the windows in our house and not want to talk to anyone. Sometimes I would lock myself in the bathroom, hide behind the shower curtain, and not come out for hours. It was my conscience. I was miserable. I even thought about suicide.

"I Was Determined to Find a Solution"

I was determined to find a solution to my problem, or I was going to end it all. I know that's a terrible thing even to consider. But the old devil had me in a corner, and he didn't let up. I'm more convinced now than ever—that's just where he wants to corner us Christians. None of my non-Christian "partners in crime" were experiencing any of this pain.

I felt driven to make things right, to correct my sin. Finally, I received a solid recommendation about another attorney. A longtime pastor/friend offered to go with me and my wife to see him. As soon as we walked into the office of this fifth attorney, he looked at me and without any hesitation said, "I don't know what your problem is, but we've got to resolve it before you leave here. I can see it in your eyes, in your face—you're a desperate man."

This attorney, a wonderful criminal lawyer, was a former federal judge. On the basis on his experience—the cases he had handled over a ten-year period—and looking at my record, he said, "You have so much in your favor. You have an impeccable past. Married forty-three years, active in the community, in your church. And you're turning yourself in.

You want to make full restitution. The worst thing that could possibly happen to you is probation, or maybe house arrest. Nothing more!" I was beginning to feel hopeful—help at last!

We then went to the office of the State's Attorney. Of course, they had no knowledge of my situation or what was going on. At that meeting we were informed that the next step would take a lot of time. To prepare my case and put together the necessary portfolio (so that I could turn myself in) would require several weeks. But in short, they agreed that once full restitution had been made, the only other legal consequence for me would be, most likely, probation.

In the meantime, while preparations were in process, the prosecutor working on my case had to take an emergency leave of absence. The replacement, a young eager prosecuting attorney, picked up my case and approached it altogether differently. He saw an opportunity for lots of publicity and (in my opinion) the possibility of making a name for himself. The press picked up the story, and he went public insisting that I should go to prison for my crime.

My attorney couldn't believe it: "There's no reason to put this man in prison! He voluntarily turned himself in. He's made full restitution. Until now he's had a flawless record—never been in trouble before." He begged for probation. But the prosecuting attorney wouldn't budge. He wanted me to serve prison time—for two and half years! I was flabbergasted. My attorney demanded, "But you can't do this! Never heard of such a thing. There are people walking the streets whose crimes are ten times more serious than this man's!" My attorney's relentless efforts accomplished little.

"Lord, Don't You Care?"

I was devastated. I was thinking, "Lord, I was just trying to do the right thing! My attorney was certain the worst that could happen to me was probation. Now I'm going to jail! What's happening here? Don't You care about me anymore?"

Then I began to think that maybe the Lord was only testing me. Perhaps, when I would actually appear before the judge, I'd be given a lesser sentence. Somehow, the judge would have mercy on me. But that's not what happened.

When I stood in the courtroom for sentencing, and the judge spoke those words, " . . . two and a half years in prison. . . " at that moment, all I could see around me was darkness. I was crushed.

They gave me one week to set my affairs in order before going to prison. I went home that evening totally devastated, a broken man.

Every bad thing that I had feared might happen, did happen. The story hit the newspapers, and the publicity was awful. The writer of one magazine article really juiced up the facts. Another reporter even tried to tie me in with the Mafia, which was the furthest thing from the truth. I received bad publicity all over the country. But to date, I have never read any of the articles or looked at any of the headlines—never. My wife has read every one and has kept every one, but I've asked her, "Please, don't ever show me." I do know the story made headlines in at least seven different magazines—especially the international hotel trade journals. I was front page news in all of the South Florida newspapers. The kindest report that was printed stated, "He surrendered." All of the rest claimed, "He was arrested and charged. . . . " One article actually said that I was the kingpin, the mastermind of the whole thing!

Besides being personally devastated, this also turned out to be a very costly experience financially. Including the five attorneys, the psychiatrist, the restitution, and the court costs, the total amount was over a quarter of a million dollars. And here I was planning to retire! There was no paycheck coming in at all while I was in prison.

Thank God, I have a beautiful wife who stood by me. She's a godly woman—for years she has headed the women's prayer ministry at our church. All of this was very difficult for her. And my children and grandchildren—they were all behind me as well. And then, of course, there was my church. Without the church, I don't think I would have survived.

When I was taken away to prison, they put me in chains. "But I'm not dangerous," I said. "I'm not a rapist. I haven't physically hurt anyone." In spite of my pleas, they chained my hands—and my feet. I could only kind of hobble along.

They locked me in the back of a truck. It was so humiliating. That was in September of 1989. I was sixty-four years old. I had never been to a prison in my entire life, not even to look at one.

When we arrived at the prison, we were unloaded directly from the truck and shuttled to a cage. They made us strip down completely. It was a cold, dreary day, and we had to stand there in line, barefooted on a cement floor, stark-naked, for three hours. They were purposely rough with us. A guard came over to me and whispered, "Hey, big man, do you want to take me on?" Another guard called me "Buddha" because of my weight. He jeered, "OK, Buddha man, come on over here."

"Sir," I asked, "could you tell me what time it is?" "I won't tell you what time it is," he responded. "What do you care? What does time mean to you? You aren't going anywhere!" "Thank you," I said.

"I Couldn't Understand It"

I was a nervous wreck when I went to prison. I was under the impression that because of my crime, which was comparatively minor, I would be sent to maybe a work camp or at least a reasonably decent place. But where they sent me was right in among hardened criminals—murderers, drug pushers, child molesters, kidnappers, rapists . . . you name it. They were my bunkmates. The guy in the bed next to me murdered three people. A fellow in the next cell was called "Butcher." He had literally taken a butcher knife and carved up his girlfriend, her lover, and her dog. After he finished, he called the police, "Come and get me." These are the kinds of people they put me in with. Hardened criminals. I couldn't understand it!

Seriously, I thought the Lord had left me. The old devil crept in and taunted, "Where's your God now? He's left you alone!" And I started to believe that.

I had been at the top of the world, received so many plaudits, and then, all of a sudden, I was entirely alone. I was at the bottom of the barrel. I was nothing more than a number. Nobody could help me anymore. My wife couldn't help. My attorney couldn't help. My pastor couldn't help. I was on my own—in the Lord's hands. Like the psalmist wrote, "My time is in Thy hands."

Those initial days in prison were horrendous. For the first week I was allowed no phone calls, no visitors, no cards or letters—no outside contact whatsoever!

It was like things just kept getting worse and worse. I was assigned a cell without a mattress, with no pillow and no blanket. They said they had just run out of each of those items. The primitive circumstances were beyond belief! However, one inmate showed a little pity and sold me an old gym bag (for a dollar) that he cut into a flat piece for me to use as a blanket. (Fortunately, he was willing to wait a couple of weeks for payment. Inmates were allowed to receive only $15 per week; so one dollar was a lot of money.) Most everybody called me "Pops" because of my age.

The regimentation of prison life was much worse than anything I had ever seen in the movies. The food was worse than bad. It was mostly rice, beans, or lettuce. Rarely did we ever see ice cream or tomatoes. We never saw radishes or broccoli or pasta. They'd give us some milk, but never cream for our coffee. We were given one piece of bread—no butter. Eggs were a deluxe item that we'd get about once a month. Dessert might be an apple—never pie. A guard would watch closely whenever we'd go through the line and put food on our trays. We were never allowed too much. I lost sixty pounds in six months.

I was so distressed that I wanted to take my life. I felt the Lord had left me and life wasn't worth living anymore.

My bunkmate, Danny, was 6′6″ tall and weighed about 300 pounds. He was serving three life sentences for killing three people. This fact isn't widely known on the outside, but I soon learned that it's possible to get just about anything you want while in prison if you're willing to pay for it—drugs, alcohol, knives, whatever. In addition, a fellow inmate, serving time for dealing drugs, was actually murdered in a nearby cell. A contract had been placed on his life, and someone on the inside poisoned his food. Even in prison, there are ways to get things done. So I asked Danny whether he could get me a pill. "I don't want to live anymore," I said. "I can't handle this." "Are you sure Pops?" he asked. "Is that what you really want to do?" "I've got to do it," I said.

And so he got me a pill. I looked at it—just a small gray capsule. "Tonight," he said, "take this before you go to sleep, and you won't wake up in the morning. Guaranteed." When they shut and locked our cells doors around 8 that evening, I said to myself, "Well, this is it."

As I lay in my bunk, ready to take that pill, it was like the Holy Spirit took hold of me. It was as though the training I had received all my life as a Christian—through the Scriptures, my church, Sunday School, my godly praying mother—it all came into focus. God, through His Spirit, said to me, "Hey, it's not over. I'm here. Don't worry, Ed, I'll work it out. I'm still on the throne. Turn everything over to Me. Trust Me." That night, in the darkness of that prison cell, I prayed and asked the Lord to give me the strength to survive. I turned my life completely back to Him.

"I Sensed His Peace"

I felt His peace come over me. It was very similar to what I had experienced when I had first accepted Christ as my Savior. Physically, I was the same person, but spiritually, something had happened—I was a different person. I flushed that pill down the toilet, laid back on the bare cot, and at that moment, I knew I was back in fellowship with the Lord. I sensed an incredible peace.

The next morning Danny asked, "Hey Pops, what happened to you? How come you still around?"

"Danny," I said, "I just couldn't do it."

"Good for you," he said. "I was thinking maybe you wouldn't do it—but then, you seemed so determined."

Throughout my life I've always been kind of the independent type, but I've learned anew that God uses other people to meet our needs. The very next day, during the limited period when we were allowed to walk around the compound, a dear black brother saw me standing all alone with my head down. He came up to me, put his big arms around me, and said, "Brother, what are you looking down for? Look up!

That's where it's all at! The Lord loves you. I love you. Let's have some fellowship." When he approached me, he didn't even know I was a Christian!

He told me he had gotten saved while in prison. He didn't know my crime; he knew nothing about me. He just cared enough—about someone who was obviously hurting—to reach out to me. He walked with me to the ball field, where we sat down and talked about the Lord until the bell rang, signaling time to return to our cells. We struck up a beautiful relationship. We were able to fellowship together and encourage each other for several months. In fact, as often as possible, we would have our devotions together. I know the Lord sent him my way—to uplift me.

From that point on, I became very active in chapel services on the compound. During my stay, I met a lot of people who had gotten saved while they were in prison. Some of them were even murderers; but now, they're finding their strength in the Lord and the Scriptures to deal with life.

While in prison, I must have read Psalms 50 and 51 hundreds of times. I read them almost every day. "The mighty God, the Lord, has summoned all mankind from east to west! . . . He has come to judge His people. . . . God will judge them with complete fairness, for all heaven declares that He is just. O My people, listen! For I am your God. Listen! . . . it isn't sacrificial bullocks and goats that I really want from you. . . . What I want from you is your true thanks; I want your promises fulfilled. I want you to trust Me in your times of trouble, so I can rescue you, and you can give Me glory" (Ps. 50:1, 4, 6-7, 9, 14-15, TLB).

"Have mercy on me, O God, according to Your unfailing love; according to Your great compassion blot out my transgressions. Wash away all my iniquity and cleanse me from my sin. For I know my transgressions, and my sin is always before me. Against You, You only, have I sinned and done what is evil in Your sight. . . . Surely You desire truth in the inner parts; You teach me wisdom in the inmost place. Cleanse me . . . and I will be clean; wash me, and I will be whiter than snow. Let me hear joy and gladness; let the bones You have crushed rejoice. Hide Your face from my sins and blot out all my iniquity. Create in me a pure heart, O God, and renew a steadfast spirit within me. Do not cast me from Your presence or take Your Holy Spirit from me. Restore to me the joy of Your salvation and grant me a willing spirit, to sustain me. Then I will teach transgressors Your ways, and sinners will turn back to You. . . . O Lord, open my lips, and my mouth will declare Your praise . . . a broken and contrite heart, O God, You will not despise" (Ps. 51:1-4, 6-13, 15, 17).

Even though I had studied Scripture for years, it was interesting to me how old texts just sort of popped up from nowhere and really ministered to me. One of the psalms says, "My time is in Thy hands." And I said, "This is it, Lord. My time is in Your hands and nobody can help me, but You."

"The Lord Used My Church"

The Lord also used my church to minister to me during my time in prison. They got behind me all the way. Initially, I felt I had let everyone down and wondered how I could ever go back to the church again. I remember one day when I was paged over the loud speaker system to report to the post office. I was hoping it would be a letter from my family—that was always a thrill for me. But instead, they gave me a huge mail bag with 700 cards and letters from my church!

The postal clerk said, "I've been here for eight years, and I've never seen anything like this in my life." Some of the cards were just a line or two: "We love you. . . . We're praying for you. . . . We forgive you. . . . We're looking forward to having you back again." It was very touching. I still have that bundle of mail, and when I get a little down or discouraged, I review those cards and reread the letters. They're a great uplift for me.

As it turned out, I served six months of my two-and-a-half-year prison sentence. I was released early because of good behavior as an inmate. I was very cooperative; plus I completed some special work assignments, as well as doing other things. But those six months still seemed like an eternity.

In the last months that I was confined, they relocated me to a work camp far south in the Florida Keys. Some camps are worse than others. This one was a horrible setting. Lots of bugs. No library. No chapel. No commissary—so we couldn't buy any snacks. Of course, it had barbed wire all around, though actually the personal freedoms were a little better there. They worked us very hard. Some inmates had to clean up litter along highway roadsides or cut down trees. Others raked and picked up clutter from the beaches. They had us cleaning toilets and facilities at state parks. Since I couldn't do heavy manual labor because of my bad back, they assigned me to inventory-type jobs. I redesigned their tool room—painted it myself—even installed a recessed ceiling, something that I had never done before in my life.

During my six months in prison I learned to appreciate the little things. All those years I was in business, I experienced the best. I enjoyed the big things of life—the Cadillacs, the limousines, trips around the world, high living. I never gave these things a second thought; they just came along with the turf. But also, I never stopped to smell a flower or take time to appreciate the ordinary. So there I was in prison. Alone. One day a little duck went by with seven ducklings following behind. I watched them closely. They had such a peace about them. I prayed, "Thank You, Lord, for creating that mother duck and her little ducklings and bringing them by here at this time."

A little bird was singing in a tree, and I said, "Lord, thank You for the bird!" I watched an alligator in the lake by the prison. I responded, "Thank You, God, for that alligator!" I enjoyed watching him so much. In my personal devotions I started praying every day, "Lord, thank You for the trees and the flowers. Thank You for the sun and the moon. Thank You for the air I'm breathing. Thank You for that little duck here." It was like all of a sudden, I was appreciating so many things that before I had taken for granted.

I learned a lot about God in prison. I learned the truth of the verse where we're told: "I will never leave you nor forsake you." Now I understand the depth of those words more than ever. God was with me *before* prison; He was with me *in* prison; He's with me *now;* and He will *always* be with me!

I also learned a lot about God's character. He's a jealous

God. For those of us who accept Christ as Savior, He wants to be on the throne of our lives. He needs to be in full control in order to use us. He wants us to be able to enjoy His peace and security—to have our prayers answered. When God is not the first priority in our lives, He's jealous. And sooner or later, He'll have to deal with us about that. He'll bring us back to Himself in one way or another. That's why the Bible says, "The way of the transgressor is hard." God's ways are not our ways.

Let me say to you, if you're living in sin, or if you have an illegitimate affection, get it straightened out immediately! Don't allow it to go on until God has to allow something hard to happen in your life. Get on your knees, and get rid of it before He does. If you turn from your sin—any illegitimate affection—I believe God will heal you from it. Turn from your wicked ways, and turn it over to the Lord as I did.

"My Church Prayed'

I was aware that people in my church had been praying for me all along. I phoned the pastor just before I was discharged in March of 1990. "When I get home," I said, "I'm coming forward in the service my first Sunday back. I'm coming down the aisle, not for salvation, because I've been saved, and not for confession, because I've already confessed. I'm coming forward as a statement to the congregation that I mean business with the Lord, and to thank them for caring for me throughout this ordeal."

At the beginning of the service that Sunday morning they greeted all the visitors, and then the pastor said, "We've all been praying for someone for a long time. That someone is here today. I know you're all pleased that he's present. Let's welcome Ed Sansovini back into the fold."

I didn't expect that. But, when I stood up, everyone applauded. In my heart, I said, "Lord, I'm finally home." Then at the close of the service, during the invitation, I went forward. My wife, Jeanne, joined me. Together, we walked to the front, hand in hand.

A few times I've been asked, if I had it to do over again, knowing all that I know now—the public humiliation, the inhumane prison experience, the cost to me financially, also the cost in terms of my reputation, the toll that it's taken on me physically, as well as the stress on my family, and on and on—in light of everything, would I still turn myself in? I don't even have to think about that answer. Yes, I would! Definitely. It was a difficult and painful thing to do. The long drawn-out process was excruciating. But, nothing could surpass the peace I now have—plus, the enjoyment once again of being in fellowship with God and other believers, and the sense that my life is really straightened out. Yes, knowing even from this vantage point all that would happen to me, I would still go through it again to make things right.

I can now sit in church, occupy a pew, and hold my head high. I'm forgiven. All is well between my Lord and me.

Something that happened shortly after I was released sums up all that I've experienced. I was speaking with an unchurched business acquaintance who has known me for years. "Ed," he said, "you've been through the highs and lows of life. You've been on the top of the mountain; you've been down in the valley. What one or two lessons have you learned from all that you've gone through that you want to pass along?" I'm sure he was expecting some significant insight related to business, but I immediately responded, "Very simply, it's a spiritual truth I learned as a kid: Jesus loves me, this I know. For the Bible tells me so."

He was stunned, saying, "No. No, I'm asking for a *great lesson,* a truth someone can hang on to." I said, "I've just told you. That's the greatest truth I've ever learned—more than any other—Jesus *really does* love me, and He loves you too!"

As I look to the future, I really don't know what's ahead for me. When I was released from prison, I asked, "Lord, now what? What's going to happen? I've been disgraced in my industry, and probably no one will ever want to hire me." But God seemed to say, "I'll take care of you. Don't worry, I'm in control."

Then along came some assignments, some consulting work. I received a personal call from Pat Robertson in Virginia Beach. He needed help to develop the new hotel, The Founder's Inn and Conference Center, on their campus. "I've heard about you and your reputation," he said. "Could you come and help me with this project?"

My wife and I flew up to meet with Pat to discuss the possibilities. Early on in the conversation I said, "I want you to know something about me." I told him about my sin and my prison experience.

He listened to my story and then said, "The Lord's forgiven you. You've made things right. It's under the blood. I'll never bring it up as long as we're together." I worked with him for a year and a half on that project as executive consultant. We took the project from beginning to end—staffing, marketing, media, the whole bit. As we filled the various positions needed, I would back off more and more, finally concentrating strictly on the marketing aspects. We had numerous luncheons and dinners; we were in lots of meetings . . . and never once did he bring up my past. He gave me the most beautiful working experience I've ever had as a Christian.

One day, while in Virginia Beach, I received a phone call: "This is so-and-so. I'm a reporter. I understand you are with Pat Robertson. We want to do a story on his new hotel." I said, "Fine."

"How many rooms does it have?" she asked. "Two hundred and forty-nine," I answered.

"How many meeting rooms?" I responded to that question as well.

Then she said, "Let's talk about why you went to prison." As it turned out, she was with one of those scandal tabloids. Needless to say, I didn't continue the interview.

Pat Robertson stood by me whenever something like this would come up. He was a great inspiration to me. In fact, he modeled for me how a Christian should act toward another brother who's been in trouble. I finished my contract with him in August of 1991.

"Doing the Lord's Work"

Because of that experience, I've decided to spend the rest of my working days doing the Lord's work. Right now I'm waiting for what that might be. I don't have the answer yet, but I know that when we ask anything in His name, He's going to supply it. I'm asking for that, and every day I'm praying, "Lord, thank You in advance for the job You're going to give me." Any day now, I'm expecting to pick up the mail, or the phone will ring, and I'll have the job I'm trusting Him for. I've claimed Psalm 37:4-5, "Delight thyself also in the Lord; and He shall give thee the desires of thine heart. Commit thy way unto the Lord; trust also in Him; and He shall bring it to pass" (KJV).

In all, there were sixteen people involved in the kickback scam. Only eight were indicted. The other eight went free without any conviction or restitution. Ironically, they were the worst offenders—they received the most money. For a while I was bitter, but now the Lord has removed that bitterness, and I pray for them. God tells us to forgive and pray for others. And I'm doing that.

As for me I'm forgiven, and my house, we're living for the Lord. Thank God for 1 John 1:9. He is faithful, just, and forgives. Praise His name!

❁ ❁ ❁

Jesus Is with Us in Trouble

"Jesus loves me, this I know . . . " is the most basic, profound truth anyone can ever learn. Jesus loves each of us so much that He died for us. He loves all of us enough that He'll stay by us in our trouble—no matter what! His love remains constant and unconditional. In fact, there's nothing that any of us has ever done or that we could ever do that will cause Him to love us less (or more!) than He does right now. That's a marvelous truth! "Jesus loves me, this I know . . . " is something both Valerie and I learned as children, but we're continuing, in these adult years, to grasp its meaning.

Neither of our parents ever had much money. Our homes were decorated with secondhand furniture and garage-sale finds. So it was a major big deal when my parents purchased the only store furniture I (Valerie) ever remember. It was a kitchen set—a gray formica table with four black iron chairs with red plastic seats and backs.

It was practically right off the delivery truck when I wrecked it. I was only eight. I was baby-sitting my younger brother and lit a match. I blew out the match and placed it on Mom's shiny-new, bought-by-sacrifice, once-in-a-lifetime table. I was shocked when, a few minutes later, I picked up the supposedly "dead" match to find it had burned a trench clear through the gray formica to the pressed wood beneath.

I knew better. I wasn't allowed to use matches at eight years of age. But I thought my parents wouldn't know what I did in their absence. Now I would be found out. I couldn't hide the evidence of my disobedience. Fear of their return gripped me.

That feeling, however, soon gave way to deep remorse. I had destroyed my mother's prize! I went from dreading her return to wanting her to come home immediately. I needed to tell my parents how sorry I was. I wanted their discipline because I knew I deserved and needed it. I wanted to do penance to make up somehow for my terrible disobedience.

I was actually relieved when they came back. I was also terribly puzzled when my punishment wasn't more severe. I had pictured the spanking of my life, or having to wear a sign for the rest of my days that announced, DISOBEDIENT CHILD! I was sure they wouldn't love me anymore—that they would wish I had never been born. But, instead, they gave me a lecture about the dangers of disobeying, especially when it came to playing with fire. My father spoke tiredly and quietly, while he dug out the blackened formica with his pocket knife. My mother cried sad tears. I received mercy, instead of justice, that day. However, I did "emotional penance" in guilt feelings for a couple of decades! That scarred table remained in the kitchen all my growing up years. They could never replace it. I could never forget it.

I learned two lessons that day. The first was that children hold a terrifying power in their parent's lives. I had made my parents very sad. I had made my mother cry, and I exhausted and disheartened my father. They were emotionally penetrable. I had pierced them. That was a most frightening piece of news.

Second, though I had this terrifying power, it didn't change how they felt about me. They loved me still, through their sadness. That was very, very clear. Otherwise, they probably would have, should have, gone to drastic measures to discipline me.

On the spiritual level, we are also "powerful" children. Our disobedience affects God. We can make our Heavenly Father incredibly sad. We can pierce and grieve Him when we disobey Him. When we ignore Him, we condemn Him to loneliness. Our sins cost our Heavenly Father. He can't, and won't, ignore sin in His children.

Still, in spite of the pain we introduce to His life, He loves us. C.S. Lewis wrote of this love in *Mere Christianity:*

> Though our feelings come and go, His love for us does not. It is not wearied by our sins, or our indifference; and, therefore, it is quite relentless in its determination that we shall be cured of those sins, at whatever cost to us, at whatever cost to Him.

Scripture gives us a wonderful picture of God's forgiveness in the Parable of the Prodigal Son. God is open armed at the curbside waiting to embrace all sons and daughters who need to come back home. That's true.

He, however, is more than just passively waiting for us to turn our lives around. This "Hound of Heaven" is actively pursuing us. He is on our sin-trail. He's created within each of us a conscience, so we can experience guilt; not because He has a sadistic streak, but because He knows we must deal with our sins. Otherwise, they exact an emotional penance that can never be paid. It is His kindness and love that exposes our sins in order to restore our self-respect and spiritual health.

Our culture is in denial and delusion about the reality of guilt. True, there is bad guilt—false guilt. But there is also good or legitimate guilt. Genuine guilt (that's divinely inspired, and not just self-imposed) persistently drives us back to confession, repentance, and fellowship with God. It was never meant to be ignored, shoved aside, or minimized. Wanting to rid ourselves of guilt, or that longing for a clear conscience, is the way God woos us back to Himself—sometimes, even at a cost of great pain in our lives. Only when we have properly dealt with our guilt—by owning up to our sin and sincerely asking God to forgive us—will God restore our dignity and sense of self-worth. Once we've taken this step, we can appreciate what it means to experience His eternal arms around us and His words: "Welcome home."

Each of us must look our guilt square in the face. We must see it for the evil it represents and be repulsed by the sin that causes it. We must tear the roots of sin from our heart. Though our sin always wounds our Heavenly Father, the Apostle Paul says, "But God demonstrates His own love for us in this: While we were still sinners, Christ died for us" (Rom. 5:8). So in light of our sin and the pain we've all caused Him, we agree with Ed Sansovini—the wonder of this great truth only intensifies: "Jesus loves me, this I know. . . ."

CHAPTER FOUR

WHEN LESS IS MORE

Jim and Cindy Judge

Watch out! . . . a man's life does not consist in the abundance of his possessions. . . . Life is more than food, and the body more than clothes. . . . For the pagan world runs after all such things, and your Father knows that you need them. But seek His kingdom, and these things will be given to you as well. . . . Sell your possessions and give to the poor. Provide purses for yourselves that will not wear out, a treasure in heaven that will not be exhausted, where no thief comes near and no moth destroys. For where your treasure is, there your heart will be also.

Luke 12:15, 23, 30-31, 33-34

Beware the barrenness of a busy life.

Socrates

Sacrifice is not giving up things, but giving to God with joy the best we have. We have dragged down the idea of surrender and sacrifice; we have taken the life out of the words and made them mean something sad and weary.

Oswald Chambers
The Love of God

You know the routine. Your daytimer is overscheduled and filled to the point of being illegible. Your children's lives are worse. Every schoolteacher, coach, private music instructor, and church youth leader wants their undivided loyalty—150 percent commitment! Family meals are rarely Rockwellian—if you manage to eat together at all.

Life's pace never lets up. You're aware of the emptiness of it all, but you don't have the energy to swim against the hectic societal stream.

Have you ever wished for more meaning, more genuine connecting within your family relationships? Ever wished for more control over your commitments and time? Ever wished your financial resources weren't already spent even before your paycheck is deposited at the bank? If you've answered yes to any or all of these questions, then you'll be interested in how one couple took back their lives.

We want you to meet Jim and Cindy Judge.

Jim is a very popular family physician in Chicago's western suburbs. He's a caring father, an excellent Bible teacher, and a man with an endearing sense of humor.

Cindy, formerly on staff with Campus Crusade for Christ, is a mother and an enthusiastic believer with a real heart for ministry. She loves people dearly. In addition, she has a wonderful adventurous spirit.

Until recently, they lived in a big "doctor house" with a pool in the right part of town. It was the "House and Garden" American dream house that most people spend a lifetime working so hard to attain.

But Jim and Cindy had a problem. They were restless. They were in crisis—a crisis of meaning. In the following pages they describe their particular struggle.

❁ ❁ ❁

JIM: On the outside, we didn't look very much like a family in crisis. Everything appeared stable. To most people we probably gave the impression of the ideal family with children involved in all the normal things. Our names never would have turned up in the church bulletin for prayer along with those who had health problems or crisis situations, but we were in crisis just the same.

I think too many good things characterized our lives. Everything was too much. All of us had too many time commitments. Our three preteen girls (Emily, Katie, and Jenny) were into everything—church activities, school activities, friends, sleepovers, organized sports like soccer and, for Emily, gymnastics . . . and when I say gymnastics, we're talking about three-and-a-half hour practices three nights a week, as well as a match every other weekend that would typically be at a location at least two hours away. It was always an all-day affair! And then there were the piano lessons with the seemingly endless repertoires and recitals to attend. They were all good things, but it was too much.

CINDY: We lived in the van! I know there's a certain amount of that with kids the ages of our children because they need to be driven everywhere, but I felt it was way out of line.

Of course the girls didn't seem to feel this way. They had no understanding that there could be more to life than just passing by each other in the hallway.

JIM: Our eleven-year-old Emily was becoming a phantom. She didn't eat supper with us except three nights a week, and she was only in the fifth grade! There were just too few evenings that all of us sat together as a family for a meal.

Time became such a stressful factor for us. Another stress point was our house.

"A Great Old Place"

CINDY: Our house was sixty-five years old, and it always needed something. It was big, and just the upkeep was difficult. It was one of those all-consuming houses. In a lot of ways it was a great old place. It was fun to entertain there, but then we began to feel like it was the expected thing to do. We didn't even feel like we should be at our pool unless we had a pack of people with us. It was sort of "Grand Central Station." Much of it was our doing. We chose that kind of lifestyle because we love to entertain. But it became too much of a good thing. It also became an enormous financial burden. It seemed like all of our money was going into the house just to keep it functional.

JIM: Every few months we'd have to spend another thousand dollars on some major project. I'm not exaggerating!

CINDY: I remember one time when Jim was so disgusted that he said, "Cindy, you can't even imagine how much we paid the plumber this past year!"

We used to really enjoy giving more, but with the demands of this house, there was no money left over to give away. Even when some ministry crisis came along, we couldn't respond—because we were living at our financial edge. We enjoy giving above and beyond our tithe, but there was no freedom left to support that kind of ministry.

JIM: In the fall of 1989 the two of us started talking seriously about moving to another house. For several months Cindy had already been saying she wanted to move into a smaller home. Initially, I wasn't very responsive to the idea. But, as usual, Cindy had figured it out first. She's much more clever and spiritually sensitive than I am. She held her tongue, while waiting and watching for me to come along.

During this period, one of the preaching themes at our church was on downward mobility. The pastor focused on truths from the second chapter of Philippians and the "Sermon on the Mount." He challenged us to build into our lives the principle that "less is more." Fewer commitments, less financial bondage, result in more freedom—more ability to be spiritually spontaneous.

I guess everyone already knows about upward mobility. It's such a suburban yuppie thing. And at that time of our lives, we were also at the end of an era nationally—the Reagan years—the years of excess. So the emphasis of this particular sermon series was of special interest to me.

I began to question the true value of the things I was giving attention to. The house wasn't just financially consuming: It was consuming in terms of my time and energy. Every season of the year was demanding. In the spring the pool had to be opened (which was a huge project!); all summer long it had to be maintained daily. In the fall we had to rake leaves—and I mean lots of leaves! In fact, every year we filled over a hundred lawn bags. Then in the winter, with corner lot sidewalks and two different driveways, there was plenty of snow to shovel. There was always something. I had overlandscaped the place. Just to keep up with basics, I had to get up every day at least by 6 to water the gardens so I could still make my hospital rounds and arrive at the clinic in time for regular appointments.

I remember asking myself, "What are my kids going to remember about me?" I could just imagine them saying, "Oh yeah, wasn't he the guy who did our yard?" I kept thinking that I only had six or seven more years with our oldest daughter, Emily, before she'd go off to college. It became clear to me that these were key years we were living.

On a professional level I was finding less meaning as well. Within me was an undercurrent of bondage and boredom. Bondage to too many commitments and boredom . . . wondering if what I did on a day-to-day basis was really changing anything. I see thirty patients a day. I go from room to room almost nonstop. In our society it's incredibly rare to have someone to talk to. Therefore, although chest pains are listed as a cause for a visit to the doctor, in reality, chest pains can also be caused by the stress of an extramarital affair . . . or whatever! And patients want to talk with me about all of that. Apart from medical concerns I end up hearing about financial problems, work pressures, marital struggles, wayward children, whatever's going on—and often, there's something else going on! All of this drained me. At the same time it was OK because that's a part of my giftedness. But I then began to realize that it was taking a toll. I was paying a price for that burden.

"We Needed to Step Outside Ourselves"

CINDY: I also realized that more often than not, Jim was coming home from work emotionally spent. He needed time alone to charge back up. He needed more free time to himself.

Personally, I was struggling with the awareness that too many of our resources and too much of our time and energy were just being spent on us. I had a growing conviction that we needed to step outside of ourselves, to take some risks, experience a real sense of God's pleasure from trusting Him more.

In December of 1989, a friend told us about an opportunity to minister in Africa. A missionary hospital in Kenya was in need of temporary replacements for several doctors who were going home on furlough. We've always had a love for missions, and I just thought there was a possibility we could spend an extended time as a family on the mission field. It seemed like a dream come true to me.

The more I thought about it, the more it sounded like the very thing—in every way—to get back on track with our kids, our values, our priorities, our lives. Doing something like this would force us to drop all of our commitments. It would give us a fresh start away from all entanglements.

JIM: But, practically speaking, it seemed impossible at first. How could we finance such a dream? How could we go an entire year without any income? The thought of going to Africa was attractive, but how could we arrange it and make it work?

Another major factor in how God was leading us came as a result of a sermon we heard at church. The pastor had been challenging the congregation (which is customary at our church) to give above and beyond during the month of December. The phrase he used was: "Give a costly gift—an amount that reflects what God gave you when He gave His Son." I couldn't get that phrase out of my mind.

After several days of processing all of this, it finally came together in my thinking: "Downward mobility. Downscaling. Snap! That's it—the costly gift would be ourselves!"

Cindy and I looked at each other and said, "Why not?" They needed us in Kenya for one year, beginning the following June (1990). We could live in one of the doctor's homes who would be away on furlough.

We were aware a decision like this one could cost us really

big. Time, financial security, our reputation—there was some risk involved in telling the medical clinic what we wanted to do. (We were already short-staffed as it was, and I knew my absence from the clinic would leave a major hole that others would have to fill.) But what we should do had become very clear!

So we decided to sell our home, go without salary for a year, and live off the proceeds of the sale.

CINDY: Even before we made this decision to move to Africa, we had already put our house on the market for a few months to see whether we'd get any bites. In the meantime we had been looking at housing all over Wheaton (Illinois). At one point we were only one day away from signing a contract to build a new house—a smaller one—but neither of us had had any peace about it. So we put the decision on hold. Looking back, I know God was at work in our lives. Then, when this Africa opportunity came up, and once we decided to go, we said, "Now it all makes sense!"

JIM: There were many reactions to our decision. Most people just kind of looked at us like, "Isn't that nice?" They had difficulty relating to it. I was most surprised at the response from some in the Christian community. They were full of questions—"Well, how can you do that? But, what do your kids think about this?"

CINDY: One girl from church just looked at me and said, "You mean, you're going to sell your big beautiful house and put everything in storage? Isn't that going to be a hassle?"

"Never a Negative Response"

JIM: There were a lot of funny reactions. But one of the miracles, one of the greatest things, was our children's attitudes. From the moment we told them what God was leading us to do, never once was there any kind of negative response. NEVER!

Another major concern where I saw God's provision was at the clinic. Seemingly out of nowhere, three other doctors showed up and were hired. So the year we were planning to be away, they would have more help than ever! All the things we initially worried about were falling into place one by one.

There was just one final key item that had to happen. As the months went by, we were unable to sell our house. And this wasn't optional. We needed to sell in order to finance the plan. To get the cheapest rates possible, we went ahead—by faith—and bought our nonrefundable plane tickets. Over five thousand dollars worth of flying for the five of us. But still, no one had even made an offer on our home.

To be honest, I had intermittent faith and panic. I'd go back and forth between, "I'm certain this is what God wants us to do," and, "Why isn't something happening here?" I thought, "How embarrassing! Here we've told the whole world our plans to serve God in Africa—and now, the house isn't going to sell!"

CINDY: But isn't that the walk of faith? The harder the situation, the more we need just to trust God. Even so, selling the house was key to everything.

JIM: For a long time in the back of my mind, I had been attracted to the idea of doing something kind of insane during these midyears. There's a line from the movie *Field of Dreams* where Kevin Costner says in reference to his father, "You know, that man never did one spontaneous thing in his entire life." I distinctly remember hearing that line and thinking, "That's not going to be a statement any of my daughters can say about me someday."

So, as I mentally projected ahead doing this sort of crazy and wild family adventure, I imagined my daughters (years from now) saying to their children, "And then . . . your grandfather just sold our house right out from under us and dragged all of us to Africa!"

CINDY: Many of us American Christians don't know anything about a risky step of faith. And that was the bottom line here that made it so much fun. We actually stuck our necks out and trusted God for something outrageous. We just did it!

It's so fun to reflect because, as God often does, He came through at the very last minute. Our house sold on the girls' final day of school in early June. The closing date was only three weeks before our flight in mid-August. It was incredible. We had adequate time to pack, put things in storage, and still had a few weeks to relax and say good-bye to everyone before our plane left. The timing was wonderful! God is so faithful.

JIM: We went to Kenya, East Africa, which is right on the equator, but it's not what you might picture. Where we were—at Kijabe, about two hours from Nairobi—is about 8,500 feet high, and the weather is similar to Denver's. The skies are bright blue and clear, and it rarely gets hotter than 75 degrees. It was beautiful!

CINDY: We were working in association with Africa Inland Mission, and also with World Medical Mission. There's an English-speaking school right there on the compound, Rift Valley Academy. Our three girls just went a mile up the hill to school—and loved it! It's a boarding school, so they met lots of children from all over the world there. Many have become very dear friends.

"I Was the Expert"

JIM: In this kind of medical setting, I was expected to be the expert in whatever I was doing. I was assaulted by overwhelming needs. Suddenly I was dealing with the worst of everything—the worst pneumonia, the worst dehydration, the worst infections, and then at this point in Kenya's history . . . AIDS, AIDS, AIDS! Generally, in the Third World, people don't go to a hospital until they are intensely sick. It wasn't long before the horrible realization hit me that there wasn't anybody else to refer cases to. I was the neonatologist, the gynecologist, the oncologist, the pediatric expert . . . you name it, I was IT for a whole year! I even had to do surgical procedures I hadn't performed for years since medical school. It was a little frightening. "What if my own kids get really sick?" I thought. "I'd have to treat them!"

On top of that, almost everything I saw was the worst case scenario. It was as if the extreme medical textbook example was always walking through the door.

Just what went on in the emergency room was incredible. Every day we were sewing up people who had been hacked by their neighbors with pongas (African machetes) or had been involved in car accidents, or maybe they were injured while being robbed. I was seeing stuff that was really shocking. It was hard to realize the level of violence that was happening around us. These injuries were normal occurrences in that culture.

There's a lot of violence going on all the time. Even missionaries are targets—not because they are missionaries, but because they are Westerners. They are the "haves" in a "have-not" world. Therefore, they are in danger as well. Practically speaking, there was no such thing as a police force.

CINDY: The girls often begged to go with Jim on emergency calls. These would come in at all hours of the night, and occasionally Jim took them along. One evening, around 8 o'clock, they went to the hospital with him to see a young boy who had been kicked by a cow. In advance Jim was told that the patient might need some stitches. What an understatement! One side of this boy's mouth was ripped all the way to his ear. His face was torn wide open. That's the kind of thing he dealt with all the time.

JIM: But there was also a very rewarding sense that whatever I did to help someone was incredibly appreciated—no matter what happened. If a person's condition worsened, no one felt it was the doctor's fault. They were happy just to have a clean bed and someone taking care of them. That in itself delighted them! So there I was, working with some of the worst equipment I've ever used while practicing medicine, but getting the best results in terms of life-saving effect. On top of that, people were grateful. It was a very satisfying experience.

CINDY: I couldn't have dreamed up all of the fun and exciting opportunities that came along during our year at Kijabe. Two different times I taught a month-long Bible class to nursing students. I was asked to develop an evangelism training course for the staff, because every Tuesday in the hospital chapel they showed Campus Crusade's "Jesus" film for all the patients who were mobile.

Then they asked us to design discipleship materials for all incoming employees as well as for anyone else who might be interested. So we developed a seven-week "basics of the Christian faith" course. We had opportunities to teach that as well.

JIM: The truth is, sometimes missionary personnel are just too overworked to develop new ideas. We found them more than eager to receive any fresh input we had to offer.

CINDY: One other experience I just have to share. I can hardly believe I did this! A single woman with several children was building her own house in a nearby village. As part of the process—after building the main framework—she needed literally to "mud" the inside. One Saturday three of us women from the mission compound went down and helped her finish off her house. We were up to our knees and elbows in mud, but how satisfying it was to help her provide for her family. What an experience!

Probably our most thrilling ministry experience was near the end of our year-long stay. We were asked to teach a disciple-making course at Moffat Bible College for one term. It was a 30-hour elective. Their educational system was in English. Jim and I taught the class sessions together, and it was such a joy. We ended up just falling in love with the group of students we had. At the end of the term we were stunned when they voted us "Teachers of the Year." What a marriage booster it was for us to work together in this way.

JIM: One of the greatest benefits of this whole experience was also the unification of our family. I felt like I was given my family back. At a time when most American families are being yanked in different directions and pulled apart (and we had also been moving in that direction) suddenly it was just the five of us. We were a unit, and we did everything together. We actually had alone time, which was the most incredible gift of all. When I'd come home from the hospital, there was nothing—no distractions, no TV, no lessons, no phone calls . . . nothing. And, we had to be creative about our entertainment.

CINDY: Evenings were family times, filled with games and reading. Those are the kinds of things we used to dream of doing, but never got around to.

"A Real Support Network"

JIM: The girls became a real support network for one another. At just the time when Emily was starting to be a phantom in our family, we made the decision to go to Africa. Now she was doing everything with her younger sisters. Our middle daughter, nine-year-old Katie, particularly bloomed with this slower pace. We came to realize that she's a child who needs this quieter type of life. I believe there are a lot of children in family systems who just get dragged along in the frenzy of life. Then we parents wonder why they're so difficult or resistant. With some kids, the typical North American, fast-moving environment is unhealthy and hinders them from "blooming."

CINDY: Our three girls (ages eleven, nine, and six) would play outdoors together for hours—having fun on the swings and climbing trees. They'd come home filthy dirty and loving it. It was so refreshing to see them so happy.

The kids were also developing a worldview. Rift Valley Academy, the school they attended, was on the mission compound, and there were at least twenty different nationalities represented among the students. There was no awareness of any blacks versus whites issues, no boundaries to community. It was like attending camp all year round. The schoolchildren related to one another so well.

JIM: There were other benefits our children experienced.

Even before we left, they saw God answer our specific prayers about the house selling; they also saw Him work out our financial needs and all the details of our trip.

CINDY: When we arrived in Africa, God provided a great house for us with everything the girls needed. We had neighbors, wonderful people, who immediately welcomed us and took us under their wing. We constantly reminded the girls of how God had worked out His good plan for our lives throughout this entire experience. And they saw it for themselves. They got to see overseas missions firsthand. They saw God working in different ways in the unusual churches we attended, in the lives of the interesting people we met, and in all the cultures they were exposed to. It was fabulous!

JIM: When we came back to the States at the end of the year, we were determined to hang on to some of the things we had benefited from in Africa. I remember, reentry felt a lot like going from a normal "play" pace to "fast forward." And somehow we had to carve out a healthy lifestyle in this once again hectic culture.

We returned to the same community in Chicago's western suburbs, and the first major task was finding a place to live. We needed to purchase a house. So here we were, looking at houses for $80,000 less than the one we had sold a year earlier. Believe me, that's a lot less house.

CINDY: While we were house hunting, it was a temptation to want to creep up another $10,000 or so in what we were planning to spend, but we were determined to stay within our agreed upon budget. We had this great incentive—freedom! To be financially free, to have free time, to be free from the burden of too much stuff.

JIM: There were a lot of funny reactions once we bought a smaller place and people found out where we had moved, which is nothing fancy, though more than adequate. One of our new neighbors was really puzzled. When we first met him, he said, "But this doesn't *look* like a doctor's home!" I told him we had intentionally decided to downscale. He said, "I'm glad you told me that because I thought maybe you had had a serious malpractice judgment against you."

Besides being a smaller house, it also has a lot less property. The place we sold in order to go to Africa had a big swimming pool on a large corner lot with an additional guest house and detached garage. The former house kind of declared, "We've made it!" However, this house says, "We're just living here."

"Freedom in Our Lives"

CINDY: I guess you could say, by comparison, the house we're in now is kind of "blah." I admit there are things we'll always miss about our former house. But both Jim and I agree that it's absolutely worth it to have this new freedom in our lives. Our house payments are much less, the lawn takes one-tenth the care, and we have money to give away that we never had all those years in that big home. But best of all we have time.

Even our kids are making decisions based on the quality of life we experienced in Africa. The children have decided on their own to downscale. They're involved in a lot less. After we returned, they just didn't seem to care as much about all of the extracurricular activities, clubs, sports, and private lessons they had been involved in before. We did, however, make them start piano again.

JIM: For me, coming back and continuing to downscale has meant creating more personal time, more quiet time alone. Without the demands of an overlandscaped yard and all my former locked-in regular commitments, I have a deeper sense of peace in my personal walk with the Lord. I don't have that sense of bondage anymore. The boredom that was earlier making me so restless is now gone.

We've continued with much more family time than was ever characteristic of us before our trip. We say no to things more easily. We say no, not just because we have something else happening, but because we don't want to be out and on the go too many nights in a row.

Also, Cindy and I now have a more intimate level of communication because of that year. As a couple we seem to be more unified. We really worked well together on the mission field and that has helped solidify our relationship.

CINDY: Working together as we did in Africa was a total high for me. We'd walk back from teaching a class at the college—at least half a mile on dirt roads—and we would just laugh and laugh. It was so wonderful.

We had lots of time to talk. Too many couples just don't do that it seems. Jim would come home every day at lunchtime, and for a whole hour we might sit on the porch together. We would literally sit in the rocking chairs and talk about us, our relationship. We reflected on the past. We looked forward to the future. We talked about the pitfalls we saw in our relationship and what to do about them. Most importantly, we made some decisions about the pace of our life once we returned home. We consciously decided—before coming back—to downscale our stress levels.

JIM: During that year away I also came to understand that, professionally, I needed to downscale or set some limits in terms of personal involvement with patient problems—especially if I wanted to survive practicing medicine! Oh, I'm still a good listener. I continue to care deeply about my patients and give each one focused attention; but when I go home, I'm learning not to ruminate on all the extra "baggage" in some of their lives. I'm no longer internalizing it. I'm not churning on it for hours and hours. So this is really helping me not pay such a high emotional cost in my medical practice. But it wasn't until I stepped back for a while that I realized what a significant price I had been paying personally.

As a doctor, my tendency has always been to feel responsible for other people's lives and the decisions they make. Now, instead, I'm much more inclined to approach people with the attitude, "I'm going to be positive and give my honest input when permitted, and then stand back and leave it to God." It's a major growth edge for me. It's a practical way I can rehearse the truth that "God's in control," not me.

So now, when I go home from the clinic, I'm really home! I'm doing a better job of leaving work-related concerns at the office.

CINDY: He's right! I keep saying, "Jim, are you really OK?" I think I knew something was wrong with him before our trip, but I didn't understand all of it.

"Minimal Investment"

JIM: As a family we're all committed to the idea of doing something like this again. Every five years or so would be ideal. Maybe we won't go for an entire year, but for whatever time I can give. It's a wonderful option for most physicians, because there are hundreds of missionary hospitals worldwide where doctors go on furlough, and there's nobody available to take their place. The need is incredible! Most are just not aware of it.

Looking back, I'm actually embarrassed to think of that motivating phrase that stuck with me from our pastor's sermon: "Give a costly gift." We both get kind of red-faced about it. Because all that we've received back from this experience has far exceeded whatever effort, money, and time we have put into it. The investment was minimal compared to the phenomenal return for me and my family.

As believers, each of us needs to be available to God. Too many of us (especially in North American culture) are spent to the max in every area. Just the thought of doing something like we've done seems impossible to most. It's probably dismissed before it's even seriously considered.

CINDY: Before downscaling, I had begun to think of myself strictly as "the chauffeur." I was amazed at the amount of confidence I regained in Africa about my own abilities and areas of giftedness—and the amount of joy and fulfillment I lived with every day. It was more than my wildest dreams or expectations. Without understanding what was going on—way back when—God planted within us a restlessness. Then along came a seed thought. Instead of dismissing it, we dared to dream. We pursued our hearts' desire—then finally, plunged in, and took a risk with God. And what He's done for us . . . well, the impact is only continuing! I'm astounded.

JIM: American believers need to get their lives back. We must learn to say no to scheduling in that last unscheduled hour of the week. We would all be less stressed out if we would just commit to scaling down in one or two areas of our lives—finances, activities, television, sports, hobbies, maybe even church, whatever. Life is short. We Christians in America need to learn to evaluate all of our commitments in the light of eternity.

❊ ❊ ❊

Overcommitment

There are more and more indicators in our society that many of us are tired of living lives strung out by overcommitment to things and schedules. Here are a few:

In her book, *Downshifting*, a national best-seller, author Amy Saltzman reports: "In a 1989 survey of 1,000 men and women conducted by Robert Half International, Inc., 82 percent of the women and 78 percent of the men said they would choose a career path with flexible full-time work hours and more family time, but slower career advancement, over one with inflexible work hours and fast career advancement. Two out of three of the men and women surveyed said they would be willing to reduce their work hours and salaries by an average of 13 percent in order to have more family and personal time, and just one-third said they would be likely to accept a promotion if it required them to spend less time with their families."

Then Saltzman adds, "There is a sense that as a nation we have been operating in remote control, obediently going through the correct motions but somehow missing the point. By the end of the 1980s, there was a growing realization by exhausted superwomen and supermen that their successful lives lacked substance."

The *Chicago Tribune* ran an article by Jessica Seigel (Sunday, March 29, 1992) titled "Possessed." It's a report on the psychology of possessions: "... experts say the current recession-induced hand-wringing has only highlighted the need to understand the clutch of materialism, which they define as the tendency to value things rather than people."

"America is indeed more thing-oriented than other Western nations: Statistics show that we spend three to four times as many hours a week shopping as our European counterparts, according to Juliet Schor, author of *The Overworked American.* As a major leisure activity, shopping has taken on the characteristics of a sport in America."

The experts are finding that the message is an old one, however, "Money doesn't buy happiness."

"High materialists are not only dissatisfied with their possessions and income, but also less satisfied with their family relationships and the amount of fun they have," said Marsha Richins, an associate professor of marketing at the University of Massachusetts at Amherst. "They certainly are less happy with all aspects of their lives."

"Everything has ground to a halt," says Grant McCracken, an anthropologist who heads the Institute of Contemporary Culture at the Royal Ontario Museum in Canada. "We know the 1980s are over. We know the yuppies are over, and we're waiting for the world to begin again. We're essentially waiting for a new set of objects to go with the new set of ideas."

In a recent *USA Today* (April 17, 1992) column, quoting from Mark Gerzon's book, *Coming into Your Own:* "If you find yourself with too much clutter, you are not alone. Many people... are reaching a 'fundamentally different stage.' ... 'The party's over,' says Peter Siris, who analyzes retail and consumer trends for UBS Securities. He continues, '... those who are entering the second half of life are changing their spending patterns fundamentally. It's not just that they're cutting back. They are trading down. For thirty years retailers have upscaled ahead of the consumer. Now the consumer may be downscaling ahead of the retailer.' Particularly for the part of the baby-boom generation who took for granted the expanding postwar economy of affluence, it is hard to come down to earth again. (As one chastened yuppie confides: 'You come to realize that you will never achieve the standard of living you had in junior high school.')"

Alexandra Stoddard, author of *Living a Beautiful Life,* writes, "Thoreau spoke of scaling down. Many wise people beside Thoreau preach simplicity. By not overextending ourselves we avoid fragmentation, clutter and nonsense. Life is too short for you to be the caretaker of the wrong details."

Even an article published recently in a woman's fashion magazine (a most unlikely source!) emphasized that scaling down is not denying yourself, but finding a balance in your life. The key point that was made: Scaling down is a gift you give yourself. It's the stress-buster for the nineties.

But for the believer downscaling must go beyond living smart. It has to be more than finding a way to survive and extricate oneself from the hectic pace of American living. For the Christian, downscaling has decidedly kingdom overtones.

We're proud of the way the Judges modeled this concept in their choices. Scaling down is making your resources, your time, your abilities, your very self available to the Lord. It's guarding a reservoir of self and then letting God stretch that part for use in His kingdom.

It's living away from the financial edge, so that you have the freedom (and can experience the joy) to contribute to God's work, ensuring that ministries that are making a difference will be able to meet the needs of a lost and dying world.

Downscaling is guarding your resources so you have something to give when someone nearby is needy or in crisis.

Downscaling means setting limits—even ministry limits. It finds quiet space with God to be still and hear His voice saying, "Be available. Be available to Me."

Downscaling. It's finding spiritual balance in a world spinning out of control. It's finding meaning for living, not in the abundance of possessions or busyness, but in the sense of God's pleasure with our choices.

Jim and Cindy Judge have a delightful embarrassment at the kudos received from their downscaling sacrifice. They know that what they had intended to be a costly gift, what seemed to others a sacrifice, has surprised them by giving them back not only their lives, but also immeasurable joy and peace, and immense satisfaction as well.

CHAPTER FIVE

A GOD OF EXTREME UNDERSTANDING

Pamela Wexler-Smith

You have seen me tossing and turning through the night. You have collected all my tears and preserved them in Your bottle! You have recorded every one in Your book. . . . This one thing I know: God is for me!

Psalm 56:8-9, (TLB)

The Christian doctrine of suffering explains, I believe, a very curious fact about the world we live in. The settled happiness and security which we all desire, God withholds from us by the very nature of the world: but joy, pleasure, and merriment He has scattered broadcast. We are never safe, but we have plenty of fun, and some ecstasy. It is not hard to see why. The security we crave would teach us to rest our hearts in this world and pose an obstacle to our return to God: a few moments of happy love, a landscape, a symphony, a merry meeting with friends, a bath or a football match, have no such tendency. Our Father refreshes us on the journey with some pleasant inns, but will not encourage us to mistake them for home.

C.S. Lewis
The Problem of Pain

Maybe it was her three adorable children. Or her horse farm. Maybe it was that she was beautiful and well cared for. It just seemed like Pam Wexler was living the "American Dream."

Back in the early 1980s, I (Valerie) taught her children music in a private secular school in South Florida. Since there weren't a lot of believers there, I was delighted to learn that this attractive family of five were committed Christians. Our families soon became friends.

Through the years we've enjoyed getting to know this charmingly eccentric woman. She's a registered nurse, a very bright and creative thinker—and, she's a soft touch for any stray animal! We often laugh at the incredibly ugly dogs and indolent cats that have turned her home into an animal shelter. She calls them names like: "Precious" and "Peaches" and "Pretty Woman"—and one particularly strange looking striped mongrel, "Camouflage Dog." We're talking UGLY! In total, there are thirteen cats and four dogs. She loves and babies each one, regardless of their natural beauty.

Pam's real love, however, is horses. Both of us have often wondered how such a petite woman can manage such large animals. But she does, and she has the ribbons and medals to attest to her equestrian abilities.

Our two boys love to visit her home in the lush mountains near Highlands, North Carolina. It bursts with life. A kid-friendly pony hangs its head over the trampoline while children jump until they are sweaty and streaked with dirt. The chickens, dogs, and cats are generally accepting of one another, having long ago established their pecking order. It's not unusual to have all the neighborhood dogs there at once. And topping it all, in the pasture, are Pam's beautiful horses.

It's hard to imagine this place ever entertaining anything besides life. It's hard to imagine that death has called at this home. And so, her story follows.

❧ ❧ ❧

"He Was a Wonderful Dad"

In 1984, we were visiting our summer home in Highlands, North Carolina. I remember looking at my husband, Howard, and thinking that he seemed unusually pale. I already knew he had lost some weight. He had expressed to me that he had been feeling very tired lately.

After a week, he headed back to our home in South Florida, where he practiced medicine. The children and I planned to stay in the mountains for another month. Once my husband arrived home and went back to work, he had a series of tests done and found out that he had colon cancer.

Howard was just forty-four years old at the time. When he had his surgery (within days of the tests), they found the tiniest tumor, but it had already metastasized throughout his gastrointestinal system. He took a series of chemotherapy treatments, and he even worked while all of this was going on, but he became progressively debilitated.

He died seventeen months later, in January 1986.

He was a wonderful dad—the best father in the world! He left behind three heartbroken children: Muffy, age seven; Seth, age ten; and Nu, age eleven. I was widowed at the age of thirty-eight.

Howard tried very hard to protect them from his pain, which probably wasn't very healthy now that I review it in retrospect. The children adored their father and were absolutely devastated when he died, especially our little girl who was the apple of his eye.

Personally, I was very confused after the death of my husband. I had never before balanced a checking account. I had never previously been involved in our legal matters. I had never taken care of anything, except the nurturing needs of my family.

"Vulnerable and Overwhelmed"

After Howard died, I was vulnerable and overwhelmed and under a tremendous amount of stress. I just couldn't seem to get it together. I lost weight. I didn't feel well. I assumed it was the stress of his death. After six months had passed—having continued like this without any change for the better—I ended up going to the same doctor Howard had seen.

I was told that I had leukemia—acute myelocytic leukemia.

Within a week I was sent to the University of Washington

Hospital in Seattle for a six-month series of severe chemotherapy treatments. It all happened so quickly!

But I can honestly say that during that time I felt the sustaining grace of God, the Father. He orchestrated all the details that had to be covered. My sister, Vivian, quit her job and moved into our South Florida home to stay with my children. (She actually did this for an entire year!)

While in Seattle I endured the most severe type of chemotherapy possible. I was told it was my only possibility for a cure, though not a very hopeful one. Many people don't even survive the treatments, let alone the disease. I lost my hair, my eyebrows, my eyelashes, and my fingernails. I vomited continuously. It was a holocaust experience.

And I had no husband.

There were several very low points during this period in my life. Just thinking of my children was agonizing. They were 3,000 miles away, and I grieved for their presence. How I longed to see them! I begged God to make it possible for me to be able to take care of them and raise them. I was very aware that they could become orphans.

I distinctly remember another low point. I looked terrible. I looked like I was dying. The doctor even said there was a good possibility that I would. The chemotherapy was so toxic and so systemic that it was excreted through my tear ducts. It affected my vision. I remember one morning trying to read my Bible, and I couldn't. That was an all-time low. I layed my head back on the pillow and cried. I finally closed my eyes and fell asleep for a short time. When I woke up, I tried to lift my head from the pillow, but the tears had encrusted on my cheeks. When I turned my head over, it tore the skin right off my face. At that moment I just wondered where God was.

Of course, the enemy wanted me to feel totally abandoned. And I did. I can say in all honesty that there's nothing spiritual about profound suffering. I didn't feel as though I was in some kind of ecstasy surrounded by a host of angels. I felt exactly like I looked—like I was dying. But deep in my heart I also knew that the Lord was there. I remember saying to Him, Job's words: "Even if You slay me, I will still trust You." That conviction stayed with me even then.

God was doing something in my life that I didn't understand. Something was happening to me spiritually. It was like God was refashioning me, piece by piece, without any calculated effort on my part.

I pleaded for my life. "Please allow me to raise my children to a committed relationship with You, Lord. Let me see evidence of You in their lives. May I even see my children's children realize who You are." He graciously heard and is answering that prayer.

Even in recovery, however, there were still many issues and spiritual struggles. I remember one Sunday going to church with my children. I was wearing this terrible blond wig. I felt so ugly, so awful. I looked around and saw all the intact families. Mothers were there with their husbands; children were sitting next to their fathers . . . it just broke my heart. At that moment my emotional grief was as intense as the physical pain I had endured while in the hospital, thinking that my children would live the rest of their lives without their father who adored them so much.

"I Felt I Was Being Punished"

Because of my own background (I'm an adult child of an alcoholic father), I struggled with my image of God during this period of intense suffering. Oftentimes I felt like I was being punished. I would review my life and ask, "What have I done to deserve this? Are You going to be there for me, or are You going to be unpredictable and unreliable like Daddy was?" I felt a great sense of confusion then. But I continued to remind myself during those times that God is a God of extreme understanding. He knew what I had lived through in my childhood, and He knew how I struggled to perceive Him positively. In spite of what was happening, I held on to the conviction that He would be faithful and be that Father I needed.

I can't say there was any one experience that cleared this issue up for me. My suffering experience has been a process. But over time the Lord continues to prove His love and faithfulness to me.

Fear is an ongoing dangling issue in my life. It plagues me

more than anything else right now. Having been through what I've already experienced, I'm aware that I could possibly have to face it again. Thinking about the "what ifs" fills me with panic. I'm also very concerned about my children's perception of God. My beautiful 14-year-old daughter recently said to me, "The only two men who I've ever loved, Daddy and Grandpa, have died." I see the fear that she has about loving someone again.

During the past six years, I've been healthy—completely well! Meanwhile, I've been learning about God's care. It's very important that those who suffer know how God looks on them and their situation. I've been learning about His care from His Word by meditating on Scripture—plus, I keep a spiritual journal.

God always meets us at our point of greatest need. My greatest need is a father-hunger. Since my dad was an alcoholic, he was unpredictable and never there. He abandoned me emotionally. I've had to be careful (and very intentional!) not to transfer that onto my Heavenly Father.

I needed a total revision of a father-model.

I have a "visual tape" that I play in my mind and in my spirit when I'm struggling with my concept of God. This exercise or discipline has worked especially well for me in relationship to my Heavenly Father. Since I love horses, I always visualize meeting Him in the pasture. After I've worked my horses, groomed and bathed them, and turned them out, I meet my Father at the end of the pasture by the creek. I realize that I'm dirty and sweaty and wearing my horse clothes. But God says that I'm clothed with strength and dignity. Then I feel free to walk with Him and tell Him what I'm experiencing that day. Perhaps I'm reliving the horrors of the chemotherapy treatments; or maybe somebody (who meant well but doesn't understand how it affects me) has just told me an even worse leukemia story—which always sets me up for a fearful reaction. Whatever it is I'm going through, I feel free to express my pain to my Father. Sometimes, I tell Him about my goals, the dreams and the joys that my heart entertains. My Heavenly Father is very real to me. He's also very different from my earthly dad.

And the beautiful thing is, His response is never punitive. He's never scolding or preachy. My Father stops and looks into my eyes. Before He speaks, I sense His love. He says, "Pam, My precious daughter, I have loved you with an everlasting love. I have given you many good gifts." (In fact, "Goodgift" is the name of our farm.)

When my Heavenly Father dialogues with me like this, the words He speaks are always directly from Scripture. (This is a mental discipline, not just a figment of my imagination.) He tells me He knew all about me before He formed me in my mother's womb. He tells me that my fears don't come from Him because He has given me a very sound mind. He has given me power to resist the enemy. He tells me He is so pleased when I humble myself and depend on Him for everything. He also tells me that He wants me to walk in peace, and that there's a future and a hope for me. He often tells me that, if a child asks for bread, He doesn't give a stone. Now obviously, all of these truths are extracted from Scripture.

"Encouragement"

One of the most helpful spiritual exercises to me is when we who are believers speak God's Word to one another rather than just expressing our own sense of sympathy or empathy about another person's problem. I remember once when a dear personal friend, Valerie Bell, told me that she sensed God's great pleasure in my courage. That was such an encouragement! At the time I felt like I was in a great abyss. And in a sense she gave me a "word-rope" to which I held tightly.

I teach a women's Bible study at our church. Many of these women are struggling with all kinds of very difficult problems. Every opportunity I get, I tell them, "God is there . . . He is with you . . . He's in control . . . No matter what our emotions tell us, God is a Father of extreme understanding. He is walking with us hand in hand, arm in arm, whether we feel it or not."

I would say to anyone who is struggling or suffering, that no matter what your situation is, you can *trust* God. For me that means, even if my world is spinning out of control—

regardless of how it seems to me—God has my best interests in mind. He also wants what's best for my children and my loved ones. Somehow (in a way that I don't understand) He will work it out and accomplish His purposes.

In 1987 we sold our house in South Florida, and I moved our family to our summer home near Highlands, North Carolina. Then in 1990, four years after Howard's death, I met and married Geoff Smith, a dear and godly man. His humility and kindness, his care for others, has blessed us abundantly.

Last winter, another series of events interrupted our lives. Geoff developed cardiac symptoms and was diagnosed with aortic insufficiency—a heart valve that does not close properly. Coinciding with my birthday and the six-year memorial of my first husband's death, the bottom dropped out of our lives . . . again. Within this short time frame of only one week, my stepdad had a heart attack, and Geoff became critically ill with bacterial endocarditis and a vegetative growth on his heart valve. Both of these men, so dear to me, were hospitalized, and I was alone. Something had even gone awry with our mare's joyfully anticipated pregnancy, and she aborted her foal. I began to think a serial killer was stalking our family. He was loose in 1986 and was now loose again. First my husband, and then me. I wondered, "Would I be next?"

One cold, dismal night, not long after Geoff's open-heart surgery, I was feeling very discouraged and fearful. My seventeen-year-old son, Seth, and I were feeding the horses and cleaning the barn. Rarely do I express any spiritual doubts to my kids because I don't want to undermine their faith. I want to build their faith up! But on this occasion I said, "Seth, right now I'm bottomed out. What we're going through is like a deep pit. I feel like I'm barely hanging on by my fingernails, and it's hard to believe God really cares for me."

Seth looked at me incredulously and said, "I can't believe you said that!" Then he spoke these words: "Mom, all of this is just part of life. Sometimes there are a series of events that are upsetting. But then, things change."

I was dumbstruck. My own son was speaking scriptural truth to me. Indeed, the Bible really does describe pieces of our life as Seth described.

To date, Geoff's health has been miraculously restored. My stepdad has also recovered and continues to do well.

These years have not been easy, and I wouldn't want to relive them. Nevertheless, somewhere between the horror of the past and the unknowns of the future, I have become a different woman. My perspective has radically changed, for I have refocused my life on what is real and lasting.

I think a lot about God's character, about what He's really like, and about what matters to Him. Those things are usually very different from the world's agenda. I notice the pain of others, and I hurt with them—perhaps too much. I look for ways to express the enormous love that I feel for my family. As a mother, the desire of my heart has always been, if possible, to move heaven and earth so my children would never have to know pain. But through all that I've experienced these past eight years, I've also come to realize that they will never grow spiritually *unless* they experience pain.

The trites and trivias of this life are now treated as such. In many respects I feel that this suffering experience has helped me rise above life's garbage, those nonessentials that the Bible describes as wood, hay, and stubble—that which will eventually perish.

Life is tentative . . . for all of us. I want to live each day in productivity, in joy, in hope. I want to model what really counts to my precious ones. I want every day to be for the pleasure and glory and honor of my Father. "I will take refuge in the shadow of Your wings . . . [He] fulfills His purpose for me" (Ps. 57:1-2).

❁ ❁ ❁

Needed Lessons

I (Valerie) have often suspected that Pam has been a "plant" in my life—a person brought into my life by divine appointment. Steve and I watched closely as she lost her husband Howard. What a horrible ordeal! But it was only the beginning. In what seemed like an instant, she was suffering leukemia and enduring chemotherapy. We learned from her suffering. Little did we know that soon I would need to apply some of those lessons to my own life.

Within just a few years, in 1989, I received a diagnosis of malignant melanoma. I was thirty-nine. Apart from a minor operation, I never suffered intense physical pain with my cancer, but I've learned a lot about fear since that diagnosis. I share with many cancer patients that sense that the Damoclean sword is dangling over our heads. Pam has been understanding beyond words when I tell her about my struggle with fear. She's also been a good model for me with her tenacious faith and trust in God.

We are both surviving our cancers today. I say I'm in remission. Pam won't use that word. She says she's in God's hands, but we both struggle with fear. It's a daily struggle to reposition emotionally to trust God. She feels anxious about the possibility of leaving her husband and children. She dreads further treatment. I feel anxious about leaving my children motherless, knowing that, should my cancer return and spread, no treatment is effective. We live with that very real possibility. But after we've discussed it, the bottom line is always: "God is in control." Pam gives me courage to say and believe those words.

We share with each other the survival skills we're learning. She writes, "You are right, Valerie. I have developed some 'getting through' techniques. One is, I try to write a letter of thanksgiving every day. Today I had such a beautiful time with the children. It was "College Day" at Furman University. We toured the campus together and talked about all the adventures that the next four years would hold for the boys. Then, we ate supper at a, yes, 'Yuppie' restaurant—Nu's choice. On the way home, we listened to the 'oldie-goldie' station and laughed until our sides ached. I prayed that each of the children would reflect upon this day as a special memory and give thanks to our Father who arranged it all."

I share my prayer litany with Pam. My particular version of "fear-busting." Before I go to sleep, I bathe my dreams in my blessings. I pray:

> Dear God, I am a woman with cancer—who has a husband who loves me deeply.

I am a woman with cancer—whose children give me great delight.

I am a woman with cancer—who has the funniest, most loyal friends in the world.

I am a woman with cancer—who has wonderful sheets to sleep on and food at every meal, and a warm bath whenever I want one.

I am a woman with cancer—who knows how it feels to be loved by God.

I am a woman with cancer—who is mightily and overwhelmingly blessed.

I have come the conclusion that both Pam and I have actually been given a gift with our cancers—if we accept it as such. That gift is living in the today! Wringing out every drop of love and joy we can from the now. And then, being oh, so thankful, for things we took for granted before.

It's a strange and painful, yet beautiful gift.

Because of this "gift" I am more tuned in to the spiritual activity around me. Lately I've been taking notice of other "plants" in my life. They always appear human, though sometimes I suspect they're angelic. (Maybe someday I'll get up my nerve to come right out and ask, "Are you an angel?") At any rate, these plants seem to be there at a time when I'm in need of a dose of courage or an attitude adjustment.

I'm beginning to see a pattern in how God works with me.

SCENE ONE:
Last winter, I was skiing in Colorado. Well, that's an overstatement. More accurately, I was bundled up in a ski outfit, rode in a chairlift with friends to the top of a mountain in Winter Park, and spent the best part of a late morning falling in the snow with skis on in Colorado. Seriously, I've never enjoyed skiing. I don't like that feeling of speeding down the side of a mountain totally out of control. But the three men in

my family don't understand that. My two sons say, "But it's so easy, Mom." And Steve had talked me into trying Colorado. He assured me it would be less icy than any place I've been before, and I'd probably really like it. So I tried.

I should have known I was in real trouble when the ride on the chair lift took twenty minutes to get to the top! That distance translates into about a three-hour descent since I fell at every left turn, and it took me ten minutes just to get back up.

My poor friends were patient, but they were starting to say things like: "I don't think it's her basic coordination. It must just be her head!"

Fear

I knew what it was. The "F" word. Fear. It immobilized me. I was already exhausted, and there was still a mountain to descend with no way down but on my skis. "If I could just break something," I thought, "then they'd have to take me down!" Mercifully, after putting on an incredible display for my incredulous friends, a ski patrol came by. I tried to be charming, though I knew this man thought I was a genuine wimp. However, I finally talked him into taking me down the rest of the mountain.

One problem: This was such an enormous mountain that what I didn't realize was that I had only been taken to the halfway point when I was dropped off.

I still had half a mountain to go!

There are some things in life that can't be avoided. Certain situations require just somehow getting through them. Having a baby is like that—no way to have it, but to have it. Being sick is like that—you just have to endure the experience until it passes. My observation is that dying is also like that. And that's how I was feeling. At that moment the idea of skiing was about as pleasurable to me as having a baby or dying. I kept wondering, "How much longer?"

Fortunately, there was a place to eat halfway down the mountain. But after lunch, it was back to the skis. As I put them on reluctantly, that familiar feeling of panic started to come back. My toes tingled. My legs wobbled. My breathing was shallow. My teeth were clenched. My eyes were squinty. There I was, standing in the midst of some of the most beautiful scenery in the world—being a big wah-wah!

"I really can't do this! I'm afraid! Get the ski patrol again!"

My friends were beginning to lose patience.

And then I looked over to my left. There were two skiers each wearing bright orange vests. In big, black, block letters one read: "GUIDE"; the other read: "BLIND SKIER"!

This wasn't funny—or was it? Was God poking a joke at Valerie Bell's expense? These two orange-vested pilgrims weren't really skiers—they were "plants"! Graciously, well maybe not—probably the better word is, incredulously—I said, "Oh, come on! You're not really blind, are you? Tell me you're not really skiing this mountain! I don't believe this! How many fingers do I have up?"

They laughed. Oh, how they laughed at me! Then I laughed. The blind skier piped up, "You can do this! Just take it one turn at a time, nice and slow. Watch how I do it, and follow me down!"

I took up my courage and followed my blind leader down the mountain. And the rest of the way, I didn't fall once. I wasn't even afraid. The only way down the mountain was down. It helped to have someone with bigger problems leading the way.

When I finally reached the bottom, I spent the next two hours watching a large group of handicapped skiers fly down the mountain. Blind. One-legged. A few without legs at all! But with special equipment provided they were able to join right in. Every one a study in bravery, pluck, and survival against terrible odds.

I learned a great lesson that day in Colorado. God communicated to me, "The path to survival is through suffering. Take up your cross and get on down your mountain. Someone has done this before with a much more difficult time of it. You can make it. You'll survive!"

SCENE TWO:

Steve and I were recently in Kansas City's airport waiting to make a connection. We were both very hungry, but there was nothing open except a hot dog stand. And I hate hot dogs! I was disgusted at such minimal effort to supply weary travelers with basic food stuffs. I was in a snit.

We took those nasty hot dogs and flat diet sodas to the counter to pay a sum close to a king's ransom. And, as we were searching for a clerk near the cash register, I suddenly noticed (while looking down, down, down) an adult dwarf with an unusually large head standing up on a stool. He held out his small pudgy hand to receive our money. At that moment my heart softened. He worked there.

"Another plant!" I immediately thought. In an instant, it was as if God had made everything clear to me again! In my spirit He whispered, "There are a lot harder things than traveling and having to eat an occasional hot dog. This man is working at minimal wage, with a great handicap, so you won't be hungry! Maybe it's time for another attitude adjustment, Valerie Bell."

The next time I'm in Kansas City I'm going to check to see whether he's still there. I suspect, however, he was whisked back to heaven, after he completed his assignment on my behalf!

They are all around us. People who suffer incredibly. People with difficult circumstances. People with worse circumstances than our own. People who display enormous courage.

People who from their beds of suffering refuse to let go of God. People who say, "Though You slay me, still will I trust You."

Spiritual survivors. They give us courage for our journeys in faith.

It's time. Time to get on down your mountain. Whatever you're facing, take courage. Take up your own cross of pain. Get on down your mountain holding on to the conviction that God is for you. We're all on a journey heading for home, our heavenly home. Go in spiritual style. People are watching. Some are watching closely. The courage you display will undoubtedly lead the way for another.

CHAPTER SIX

IN GOD'S PARADE

Bill and Edith Rediger

Who shall separate us from the love of Christ? Shall trouble or hardship or persecution or famine or nakedness or danger or sword? As it is written: "For your sake we face death all day long; we are considered as sheep to be slaughtered." No, in all these things we are more than conquerors through Him who loved us. For I am convinced that neither death nor life, neither angels nor demons, neither the present nor the future, nor any powers, neither height nor depth, nor anything else in all creation, will be able to separate us from the love of God that is in Christ Jesus our Lord.

Romans 8:35-39

UNDER CINDY'S SPELL

Diminutive dancer, Fair-faced fairy,
Twirling pixie dust
you pranced through our lives.

Spellcaster, Charmer, Tawny child-woman,
We tried to tame you
with serious thoughts.

You blew us kisses,
Eluded us gently,
Blithe spirit
Unburdened,
Your short sweet life.

Ethereal laugher, Spinner of magic
Did you know adult things
would never matter?

Impish angel, high-stepping show-stealer
Your cocoon barely opened
When evil molested.

Now you blow God kisses,
Delighting your Father,
Praise-twirling
Throne-room darling,
Eternally home.

Valerie Bell

"The Redigers were unbelievable. I have never witnessed such control and such dignity under these circumstances. In the midst of the heartbreak and tragedy they were like a rock. They held us all up. I could see their strength came from an absolute, unshakable faith. All of this made a very great impression on me."

Detective Jim Rendell

We love being with Bill and Edith Rediger. We got to know them nineteen years ago when Steve was a youth pastor and their three girls came through our ministry from junior high on up.

There is a bond between our families . . . an attachment. They always make us feel very loved. For more than five years, Steve and Bill played tennis together in South Florida—every Monday afternoon, like clockwork. Afterward was debriefing time. It was a tradition to poke fun at Steve's unconventional, gotta-win-or-else, all-over-the-court, finesseless, but often-winning tennis style. They too are competitors.

On our part—well, we just love their family. Their oldest daughter, Tammy, is married now—has two "squinkly" little girls. We tell her that regardless of how naughty she thinks they are—she deserves it—and more! You see, we remember Tammy at all her pubescent stages. She provided us with some wonderful, funny, crazy memories. It was never dull or boring when Tammy was around. In fact, it's still not. She recycled herself into our lives five years ago when I (Steve) hired her to join The Chapel of the Air staff. Tammy now serves part time, out of our Denver office, in the area of station relations.

We had moved on from youth ministry by the time their youngest daughter had become a teenager. But, at a distance, we've watched Barbara become a bright, musically accomplished, beautiful, talented young woman as well as a wife and mother. Well-raised children are the pride of their parents. Bill and Edith have reason to be very proud of both Barbara and Tammy.

We also remember their middle child, Cindy—a spirited, winsome, attractive young woman just beginning to take form and blossom. But we will let her parents describe her. We will use our space to tell you about her parents. When Steve asked Bill and Edith to help us with this book, they were willing. In an honest moment, however, Bill called it an "unwanted honor." We understood.

Bill and Edith are both educators, not publicity seekers. And yet, for years they lived under incredible scrutiny by the press and news media in South Florida. Anything they said could, and often did, end up in print or on a newscast. It must have seemed never ending to them.

Yet, we would say, even under the most difficult of situations, Bill and Edith and their children were stellar. Dignified, composed, emotionally honest, spiritually articulate—never pushy—South Florida saw and felt their heartbreak almost daily for a while. Moreover, under the glare of the public spotlight, they also showed South Florida something else. They saw a husband and wife and their children walking with God—trusting Him—even in the midst of their questions and sorrow.

They've given us all a rare glimpse of God's grace.

Valerie and I admire them greatly. We also appreciate their willingness to relive their story, to come back into the spotlight, for just one more telling.

Thank you, Bill and Edith. You are special to us. We love you both very much!

❦ ❦ ❦

EDITH: Thursday, January 5, 1978, is a day forever stamped in my memory. Looking back (it's been over fourteen years now), I realize that what happened was such a shock at first that we were just sort of numb.

BILL: Nothing could have prepared us for an experience such as this. I remember that particular day quite well.

It was the day before my forty-sixth birthday. When I got home from work, the house was empty, which was not uncommon if Cindy had band practice. As a school administrator I usually went to the office very early, so I would typically be home in the afternoon by about 4. On this particular day, Cindy had left a note saying she would be home by 5 because she had a baton lesson. Her note ended: "I'll clean up my room when I get home!" But 5 came and went. Then my wife, Edith, came home with our youngest daughter, Barbara. "Have you seen Cindy?" I asked. "Do you know where Cindy is?" Neither of them knew.

The hours passed. Six o'clock, 7, 8 . . . and no Cindy. My initial anger gave way to concern; then, after several hours I became seriously worried.

At about 9, when she still hadn't returned home, I called the police. It appeared that we had a missing sixteen-year-old daughter.

EDITH: As those hours continued to pass that long January night, we became increasingly worried. Never in our wildest imaginations did we even consider that she might have run away. We began to realize that something very serious must have happened because Cindy was an exceptionally dependable person.

She had been spending quite a bit of time with her boyfriend John. They were both high school juniors, and both were very popular—maybe too popular, we thought at times. She was getting so busy at school. She participated in many school activities and earned better than average grades. At the same time I felt a compulsion about keeping her involved in the youth group at church.

I remember one conversation with Cindy that occurred in the doorway at our house (Bill and I were trying to be casual—not too preachy). We were talking about what a tremendous influence for good she could have through her popularity. "I would just love to see you show Christ to your friends," I said. She was a little ill at ease with the conversation and kind of grinned. "Just two more years of high school left to have fun," she said. "Then I'll graduate and have to get serious!" She went on, "All the kids know I'm a Christian. They already tease me about going to church so much. There's lots of time, Mom." I'll never be able to forget her using that phrase: "There's lots of time, Mom." This was shortly before Christmas.

BILL: We liked John a lot. He was in athletics—was a star pitcher in baseball, played football, and loved to surf. He seemed to be a very good, well-mannered, levelheaded boy.

Cindy was the head majorette of their award-winning high school marching band and the featured baton twirler. She twirled at all the halftime shows during football season. The team had just completed a very successful year, winning several postseason games enroute to the state championship. So she had received a lot of exposure throughout South Florida. She had even won a trophy in a statewide twirling competition earlier that year.

"So Special"

EDITH: She was so special. People said she was like sunshine. Cindy and John were just great kids—even the media talked about them as "All-American" teenagers. Cindy was also very active in the church. Besides attending regular Sunday services, she participated in most of the midweek and weekend youth activities, outings, and retreats. She also sang in a select ensemble. She even went on several short-term overseas missionary trips. Of all the adults in her life the ones she most admired were her youth minister, Steve Bell, and her church choir director, John Shev. She was always proud when any of her friends met either of them and they never disappointed her, always making her friends feel welcome and at ease.

As each hour went by, we just knew that Cindy had to be some place where she was unable to call us or let us know what was happening. The minutes ticked by so slowly. It was the longest night of our lives. Some neighbors came over and sat up with us all night. With the passing of every hour, it was more and more apparent that something was seriously wrong.

BILL: The police told us to come in at 8 in the morning if she was still missing, and a detective would be assigned to the case. The detective didn't arrive until about 9, and at first he treated the situation very lightly. "Lots of kids do this, Mr. Rediger. How well do any of us really know our kids?" Basically, that was the tone of the entire conversation. It was discouraging.

I returned to the house feeling desperate. Shortly after 1 o'clock that afternoon, two police officers came to our front door, and immediately I knew there was some news. John's car, a 1970 Pontiac Firebird with a surfboard rack on the roof, had been spotted by a fisherman. It was submerged in an irrigation canal on the outskirts of Boca Raton, a couple of feet from a boat ramp. The police said it wasn't an accident. It had been driven into the water deliberately—the ignition was on, and the car was in gear.

EDITH: My mind wasn't working too clearly. I was still thinking "accident," and my first questions were: "Was there anybody in the car? Could they have gotten out?" The officers were very kind and gently let us know that they were quite convinced of foul play. Most likely, the car had been driven into the canal to hide evidence. They informed us that divers would be exploring the canal bottom, and later in the afternoon dragging operations would begin.

BILL: Evidently Cindy and John did have the picnic they had planned for that afternoon because in the trunk of his car they found a grill with pieces of cooked hamburger on it. His family said he had cleaned the grill the night before. Also, a thermos of iced tea, John's shoes, and Cindy's purse were found inside the car.

During those first few days, the Boca Raton police department set up numerous search parties. They combed the area nonstop. It was an all-out effort. The police even brought in specially trained search dogs. I remember at night watching the sheriff's helicopter overhead with big powerful searchlights. They made sweeps around the community, over our house, over densely wooded areas nearby. It was hard to comprehend that "they were looking for our Cindy." That happened at least two consecutive nights. They were searching for Cindy and John twenty-four hours a day.

EDITH: On Saturday morning, two days after the disappearance, hundreds of students, parents, and family friends showed up at the Boca Raton High School cafeteria to form additional search parties. (The media reported over 500 were involved.) The police organized a massive search to concentrate on six secluded locations in Boca Raton known to be frequented by teenagers. The goal was to find some kind of evidence or clues.

BILL: That day, they did discover where Cindy and John had picnicked—they had left behind their sandwiches. So at that point, we were sure something very awful had happened. I was almost certain they had fallen into evil hands.

"Reporters at Our House"

EDITH: The news media picked up on their disappearance right away. It was headline news all throughout South Florida. By Sunday, the TV stations from West Palm Beach, Fort Lauderdale, and Miami, all had news reporters parked at our house.

BILL: The County Sheriff's department and local city police worked together very cooperatively. Large "missing posters" were printed and placed all throughout South Florida. Advertisements were put in newspapers in nearby cities. A $10,000 reward was offered for their safe return.

EDITH: We still retained some hope. Actually, I was more optimistic than Bill. I kept thinking, "These things happen to other folks. They don't happen to us. We're just ordinary people." We experienced a myriad of feelings and emotions during this time. A glimmer of hope for a moment... then disappointment... a new lead... but, it went nowhere. It was an emotional roller coaster ride that just kept going.

BILL: I was convinced—after three days had passed, and she had not been found, and we had not received any word from her—that probably she had been murdered. However, I kept those thoughts to myself. Then, one of our good friends took me aside and counseled me to prepare both my wife and our other two daughters, Tammy and Barbara, that most likely, Cindy would never return to us.

EDITH: The Sunday after the Thursday night when Cindy disappeared, the rest of the family went to church, but I stayed home in case there was an important phone call. That morning I listened to the live radio broadcast of our church service, and I remember the soloist, Dave Florence, singing "Under His Wings." I knew he had chosen the song especially for us. The words were very comforting, but I remember that was the first time since the disappearance that I just sat on the sofa and cried. However, I went back to work on Monday, as it seemed there was nothing better to do.

BILL: We brought our oldest daughter, Tammy, a freshman at Taylor University, back from college. She wanted to be home with the family, and, of course, all of us wanted to be together. But, after a couple of weeks and still no word on Cindy, the time came for Tammy to return to school.

EDITH: It was really tough for Bill and me to send her back. She struggled too. She felt all alone there. She even called the moment she arrived on campus and wanted to come back home. "Mom, I really feel this is the Lord's will. I should quit college and be with the family right now." I just prayed and prayed. In fact, I remember thinking that I was praying as much for Tammy as I was for Cindy.

BILL: It didn't seem right to encourage Tammy to put everything on hold. She needed to go on with her life. Our youngest daughter, Barbara, was in junior high. Edith and I knew we needed to keep our family going for the sake of the girls. Life couldn't stop for any of us!

EDITH: The days turned into weeks . . . and still no word. That was an extremely difficult period. But even in this time of limbo I sensed the Lord's closeness and was ministered to especially through His Word.

We also read a few books that were written for people who were suffering as we were and that provided some help.

"Thanks to God"

BILL: I honestly don't know what people do in situations like this who aren't Christians. We had to learn all over again what it really meant to trust God. There were no other alternatives! And I'm not saying that was easy.

In fact, one of the negative things that happened—a well-meaning, but thoughtless lady from church asked me, "Have you given thanks to God for taking Cindy? You know, the Bible says that in all things you are to give thanks." That was very difficult to handle. I don't think I even responded to her.

Thankfully, we had some wonderful friends who made it a point to go out of their way to keep us busy, to just be with us even though our minds were a million miles away. They helped us process what was happening, as well as think about other things—which kept our lives moving.

EDITH: As I already mentioned, the first night Cindy was missing our next-door neighbors (from both sides) came over and stayed up with us the whole night. They didn't say much, but they were there. That, in itself, was a great comfort. Another night, one of Cindy's closest friends and her mother stayed with us. Having them at the house helped get us through those long night hours.

BILL: I remember some good friends, Bob and Miriam Carlen, inviting us out for coffee to introduce us to friends of theirs who had recently lost two children. Meeting others who had gone through tragedies and grief experiences with their children somehow seemed to help. At least we knew we weren't the first to go through something like this.

Cindy and John had been missing just over a week when some friends, wanting to be helpful, invited us to go to West Palm Beach to attend a weekend concert featuring the Gaither Trio. I remember feeling very shaky about going because that would mean neither of us would be home by the phone. (We wanted to be available because the reward had just been changed. Now, $10,000 was being offered just for *information* leading to the arrest and conviction of their abductor.) However, we decided to go with our friends, but told the police where we could be reached, just in case.

Edith and I enjoy playing tennis. In fact, it is one of our recreational passions in life. When friends encouraged us to start playing again, we resisted at first. But eventually we did, though both of us felt kind of guilty about it.

The truth is, whenever friends took the initiative like this, it was very helpful because it forced us (in a good way) to keep on living. There were so many people who were reaching out to us. And so much food!

EDITH: One of my tennis friends brought over a seven-layer salad. Somehow it hit the spot. I kept asking her why it tasted so good, and she kept saying it was just plain old salad. Oddly enough, about a year and a half ago, her daughter was killed in an accident, which gave me a unique opportunity to minister back to her. "Janet," I said, "I'll never forget that salad you brought to us in our dark hour twelve years ago. And now here you are going through a similar thing. I understand your pain." It wasn't exactly a "welcomed" opportunity, but I felt compelled to reach out and offer our love in a meaningful way.

BILL: As the weeks passed, we continued working closely with the police and communicating with the news media. We were trying to be as helpful as possible in hopes of finding news about Cindy. That was an extremely stressful period. Everyone was very kind, but it was a lot to deal with.

One newspaper article reported:

> Mrs. Rediger said she is trying to take a philosophical attitude toward the family's tragedy and to keep busy to keep her mind off it as much as possible.
>
> "I try not to let myself think about it. But the longer it goes the harder it gets. If they are alive, they are not free. They are either dead or being held (against their will).
>
> "All we can do is hope for the best and prepare ourselves for the worst."

"How Can You Let This Go On?"

EDITH: Cindy disappeared on a Thursday, and I had gone right back to my classroom teaching the following Monday.

Looking back, that was really a good thing. It did keep my mind busy. However, there were some hard things about it. One day—after several weeks without any word about Cindy—during an early morning faculty devotional time at the Christian school where I taught, one of the teachers shared about asking God to remove a personal headache. This teacher reported enthusiastically that the prayer had been answered, and God had taken it away. Well, that just got to me! It made me angry. I had to get out of that room immediately. I remember leaving in a rush, storming down the hallway to my classroom, then throwing some papers off my desk, and crying out, "God, if You can take care of somebody's measly headache, why can't You answer some questions for us? Why can't we know what's happened to Cindy? How can You let us go on like this?"

Occasionally anger would surface, but at the same time I knew there were a lot of prayers being offered for us. In the past I had heard people testify about being "held up in prayer." And frankly, I didn't relate to what they were talking about. But during those weeks with so many issues still dangling, I truly experienced an uncommon, "down-underneath" peace—even though my life was in turmoil. To this day I believe that inner sense of peace was the result of the prayers of God's people. I had never felt that before. The personal support of our friends and our church, and their combined prayers, got us through this intensely difficult period.

We were kind of amazed how this crisis in our family prompted many church people to become more intimate with us and to share tragedies that had happened in their lives years earlier. In most cases we were completely unaware of their stories or situations. So the body of Christ did minister to us graciously and effectively during this agonizing time.

BILL: Weeks became months. No word. Even so, we were trying to get our lives back to some kind of normalcy. But during all those weeks of wondering what had happened to Cindy and John, we developed a habit. Though we'd be driving back and forth to work, or going to or from church, both

Edith and I (individually, or when we were together) would always be glancing at the side of the road or in the underbrush looking for their bodies.

Exactly ten weeks after they had disappeared, their bodies were discovered, quite by accident. Their badly decomposed bodies were found next to each other in a remote section of Boca Raton by a 18-year-old motorcyclist riding his new bike in the uninhabited area. He had gotten off his bike to look for scrap metal when he stumbled on the bodies underneath some foliage.

The newspaper reported him saying, "The tunnel in the underbrush effectively hid the bodies from view. You couldn't see them unless you were standing almost on top of them."

So the big question had been solved. Cindy was no longer missing. We had been suspecting the worst, and it was true—our sixteen-year-old daughter was dead.

But we still had so many doubts and unanswered questions. "Why had this happened to Cindy?" It seemed like so many young people were out on the streets all the time, doing foolish things, and putting themselves in jeopardy; but Cindy was never out like that. We asked, "Why? Who?" So many missing pieces. So many questions.

The Friday, March 17, 1978 "Special Edition" of the *Boca Raton News* reported:

> Fresh, numbing grief has smothered the cruel uncertainty that lay heavy on the people who loved Cindy Rediger and John Futch.
>
> Today begins the end of their dark questions about what happened to a sparkling girl and a golden boy who left this life after a picnic in the sunshine.
>
> Thursday night was a beginning for police, whose meager clues in the young couple's disappearance were stale weeks ago.
>
> Bill and Edith Rediger and Bob and Sally Cookman have set aside part of Sunday afternoon to lay their children to rest.
>
> Thursday, they learned from police there was great likelihood that two bodies found in northwest Boca Ra-

ton were their missing children.

In the late afternoon and evening, they watched and listened to news bulletins as the official process of identifying the pair through dental records began.

Bill and Edith Rediger were at home in Paradise Palms after police notified Mrs. Rediger of the possibility that Cindy and John had been found. Their older daughter, Tammy, was home from college when she heard the news from a careless caller.

Mrs. Rediger said, "I guess this is the end. It's a great comfort to me to know that Cindy's in heaven, and that she very likely has been since the night of January 5.

"It's possible we'll never have any more answers in this life. It helps for me to know that Cindy was a born-again Christian, and that no matter how terrified she may have been that night, she had the avenue of prayer. I know she did," Mrs. Rediger said.

Cindy's father said he had asked his wife just the night before whether there was any news in the case. The knowledge that his little girl would not come home again took away all the hope, along with the strain of uncertainty—like so much air escaping from a balloon.

"Home with the Lord"

EDITH: Shortly before their bodies were discovered, I remember reading Psalm 53:5 in my personal devotions: "There were they in great fear, where no fear was." I just latched on to that. I thought God was saying to me, "Don't worry. Everything is all right." That was just two days before they were found. It gave me some hope at the time. Of course the reality was: Cindy was already in God's presence when I read that Scripture. So in looking back with some perspective, I realize there really wasn't any fear at that moment because Cindy was already home with the Lord. I thought the verse meant something else when I first read it, but actually the verse was still true.

Learning the truth brought a big sense of relief. The thought of possibly going through our entire lifetime not knowing what had happened to Cindy was harder than knowing she was dead. I distinctly remember driving my car to deliver her picture to the newspaper right after we learned of her death. There I was, automatically looking out the car window again. But then I thought, "I don't have to look anymore. I know where Cindy is. I know she's in heaven." So that's one of the things that hit me after the bodies were found. Relief. Finality. At least we know.

Of course all along, we were still concerned about our oldest daughter so far away at Taylor University. She wasn't supposed to come home until early April. But Indiana had been hit with a terrible snowstorm, and the administration decided to close school the week before Palm Sunday. At the time I remember praying, actually complaining, "Lord, what are You doing now? She's just getting readjusted to college and beginning to experience some good things again, and now we're going to have her come home and go through this whole ordeal again?" It didn't make any sense to me.

But God knew much better than I. Tammy arrived home the weekend before Cindy's body was found. She didn't have to be taken out of classes or miss any exams. After her sister's funeral, she returned to Taylor and was able to finish out the year.

BILL: The weekend of the double funeral was kind of a blur. The service was held on Palm Sunday afternoon. The papers reported that over 2,000 people attended the combined funeral. The band from the high school was asked to play, but they could hardly make any music because of their tears. The baton corps and the baseball team were the honorary pallbearers. Rev. Burt Reed, a pastor at our church, took care of a multitude of details. Brad Margus, county student president and one of our own church youth group leaders—and one of Cindy's dearest friends—spoke of Cindy and John with great love. Rev. Steve Bell, Cindy's youth pastor, highlighted memories of Cindy and John and emphasized what all of us could learn from their lives; and then, Dr. Torrey Johnson, the senior minister, shared a powerful message that day.

According to one newspaper account the day after the funeral:

It was an odd juxtaposition of sights.

High school band members, in their brilliant blue and white uniforms, accustomed to bringing added spirit to football game halftimes, sat solemnly on stage wiping tears away with their white gloves.

No less than 30 bouquets and sprays of spring flowers decorated the front of the stage and the tops of two dark wooden caskets.

And the photographs of two bronzed, smiling youths—pictures that had no doubt graced the family foyers and found their way into wallets of parents, siblings, and friends before becoming known in newspapers and on innumerable posters—now set atop those forboding caskets.

But the strange pairing of beauty and youth with darkness was somehow fitting for John Futch, 17, and Cindy Rediger, 16.

More than 2,000 people came to remember them yesterday at a joint Palm Sunday service at Boca Raton Community Church.

They came to remember the two young people—he a promising athlete, she the school's featured baton twirler; popular high school students, young sweethearts—as they were.

And as their parents and their former spiritual counselors believe they are—spiritually whole; looking down upon the earth from a place of peace only the dead can obtain.

"It seems as though today midnight has come at noon," said Brad Margus, a Boca Raton High School student and close friend of Cindy's.

The sobs of young people resounded through the hall.

"In these past 10 weeks, Boca High just hasn't been the same without them. They were real winners, and they really loved each other too," he summed up simply. "We're really going to miss them."

But in the spirit of recovery that prevailed throughout the service—recovery for the friends and family that waited 10 weeks to learn the young couple's fate—

Youth Minister Steve Bell asked the congregation to put aside the tragedy of unwarranted death and learn from the quality of the youths' short lives.

"If Cindy and John could break through to us today, I believe they would tell us to re-evaluate our priorities," he said.

He asked listeners if they remember to show their love for family and friends. He remembered that on a church trip last summer "whenever possible Cindy would wear John's baseball cap. She looked silly but she didn't care. That was her way of showing her love."

As teens—boys and girls alike—wept, and parents sat stonefaced, knowing it could have been their children for which the prayers were recited. Rev. Johnson prayed for the moral betterment of the community.

"Only then will these two young people not have died in vain," he said.

"It Seemed Like Mass Confusion"

EDITH: During the funeral I sat in the front row and stared at those twin softly gleaming coffins with Cindy's and John's smiling pictures on top. I just couldn't believe that our beautiful, perky, in-love-with-life, laughing daughter was in there. It was very difficult. The specifics of the funeral all blended together in my mind—the preparations, the band, the speakers, the crowd of people, TV cameras, reporters; it all seemed like mass confusion to me. But the one part I vividly remember was Steve's wife, Valerie Bell, singing that powerful song, "Finally Home." I was riveted to her every word:

> Just think of stepping on shore, and finding it heaven; of touching a hand, and finding it God's; of breathing new air and finding it celestial; of waking up in glory and finding it home.

I focused in as Valerie sang and formed a mental picture of our Cindy literally experiencing the reality of those words. It's a picture indelibly imprinted in my mind. I still carry it with me and concentrate on it whenever my grief becomes overbearing.

BILL: Adjusting to Cindy's death has been a process. I began to realize that other people had gone through similar pain. Concurrent with our tragedy, there was another family in Kansas who lost five children in a senseless murder. I truly empathized with them. "How did they get through it?" I wondered. And then there was another family in Miami who lost their daughter and her boyfriend about the same time.

We received lots of letters and cards from people who had gone through similar situations. In fact, most of the people we didn't even know. I guess we received hundreds of cards during those months. People told us about tragedies in their lives and how they coped. It helped us realize that, if others had survived this kind of heartbreak, we could too.

I don't think the pain will ever go away; but I can testify that it becomes less intense. It's true. Time does heal. We're certainly doing better now than we were immediately after the disappearance. Of course, fourteen years have passed.

EDITH: For so long—months and months—I just went through the motions of smiling and saying to people that I was getting adjusted and doing all right. But then, I definitely remember a turning point. It was several months after the funeral, and I was talking to someone on the sidewalk after church. I answered a question with a smile and afterward thought, "I really do feel better." For a long time I was sure I'd never really smile again or feel any better at all. But as I got back into the flow of life, and with the passing of time, it did eventually happen.

BILL: Naturally, we often wonder what Cindy would be like today. She'd be 30 years old right now. Of course, we're curious about who she might have married, how many children she would have had, what her adult interests would be . . . so many unanswered questions.

EDITH: One of the biggest questions after the bodies were found was who had committed this crime? We couldn't figure out any reason for it. It was such a senseless murder. Just no reason at all.

BILL: Well, Cindy and John had gone on an afternoon picnic. Later we learned that they had been kidnapped from that picnic site and driven to a secluded location where they were murdered. According to the autopsy they were each killed by a gunshot to the right side of the head. But we didn't know why. We looked for those answers for over three years. The authorities and detectives who were working on the case—who stayed in touch with us—were all wonderful people. But they had no leads to go on.

EDITH: They just ran out of clues. But then, unexpectedly, after more than two years, a private detective who was working on another case came upon a lead pointing him to someone who supposedly knew who had murdered Cindy and John. He pursued it a little while on his own to substantiate that he was really on to something, then turned it over to the investigators at the Boca Raton police department and the State Attorney's office. They pursued it from there.

"Only If God Allows"

BILL: During the nearly three-year waiting period, with no leads, people would frequently ask, "Do you think the murderers will ever be caught?" And I remember thinking, "Only if God allows it to happen."

All along we thought more than one person was involved. We thought perhaps they were still in the area. However, I seriously wondered whether they would ever be caught. I was fairly certain there were people who knew what had happened, but for whatever reason didn't come forward with any information. Naturally I felt anger toward these people.

As it turned out there *were* people who knew—at least five different ones. And even though there was a $10,000 reward for information about the murderers, they did nothing about it—perhaps out of fear for their own lives.

EDITH: Over three and a half years after their murders, that clue eventually led investigators to the two murderers. They were migrant workers in their mid-twenties.

According to court documents, detectives pieced together

the following account (as reported in the newspapers):

> On January 5, 1978, [the suspects] were riding in a truck with [two other men]. The four men were returning from tomato fields and were headed to a home....
>
> As the foursome passed a large banyan tree ... they saw Futch's Pontiac Firebird, the affidavit said.
>
> Miss Rediger ... and Futch ... left school early that day to picnic.
>
> When the four men got to the ... home, [the suspects] told the others they were going hunting, and walked toward the picnic area. [One man] was armed with a .22-caliber rifle, and [the other] was armed with a shotgun, the document states.
>
> They encountered the teenagers at the picnic area, and took them hostage at gunpoint, authorities said in the affidavit. Futch drove while [one man] sat in the front seat with him, and Miss Rediger and [the other man] were in the backseat.
>
> The document says they drove to a secluded area about one and a half miles from the picnic area....
>
> Police said [one man] left the car, taking Miss Rediger with him. They walked over a mound of dirt into dense shrubbery ... [the other man] meanwhile, held Futch at gunpoint.
>
> The affidavit states [the one man] and the girl were gone about five minutes when two shots were heard. [He] then appeared at the top of the dirt mound and told Futch "he had better see to his girlfriend."
>
> As Futch scaled the mound of dirt, he was shot by [the man], police said. Futch's body was then rolled over the mound and placed next to Miss Rediger's body.
>
> The two suspects then drove Futch's car to a boat ramp at a canal ... then drove the vehicle into the water, authorities said in the affidavit.
>
> The men then walked to a nearby labor camp and got a ride back to the ... house with another laborer....

BILL: There was no question that these two men were the

murderers. The year that followed was filled with agonizing decision-making. Should we pursue the death penalty? As it turned out, the person who pulled the trigger had killed two other girls (after killing Cindy and John). His accomplice was a vagrant. Initially, we were told they would certainly put these men to death. But then the more they looked into it, they realized they didn't have that much hard evidence—just one man's testimony against the other man's word.

"Multiple Life Sentences"

EDITH: Dealing with all of the subsequent questions was no easy matter. The issues were difficult to resolve. We really agonized over the process. But we received counsel from the State Attorney's office. In the end, through plea bargaining, both men were sentenced to multiple life sentences with no consideration for parole for at least fifty years. They could come up for parole in the year 2031, but that would be just to consider parole. It wouldn't be automatic.

The judge was very explicit about the seriousness of their crimes. He was tough and fair at the same time. We felt it was handled well—and finally put to rest.

BILL: We decided not to pursue the death sentence because we didn't want to take the chance that these very cruel, unfeeling men would get off because of inconclusive evidence. It was important to us that they never be able to hurt an innocent person again.

EDITH: Our church and our friends were so important to us during this whole experience. I know I learned to trust God more. Through it all I was very concerned for my family. I felt that I would survive with my faith intact, but I wasn't certain how well my loved ones would do in the process. One thing that came out of this: I learned to pray more—and more specifically—for each family member.

Perhaps I should have been more concerned for myself. I did all right—especially those first nine months after their deaths. But I was far from healed. I stayed busy. Read books. Connected with my friends. Threw myself into my teaching.

Continued playing tennis regularly. It seemed like I was doing fine. Then in the fall—I'm not exactly sure why—I began to struggle fiercely. I didn't even tell Bill. I didn't tell anyone because I didn't want to burden anyone with more problems. Looking back all these years later, I think it was probably because Cindy's birthday was in November, and the football season had started without their star twirler. Plus, we could hear the marching band practicing from our home.

It was a time of terrible depression for me. I began to fantasize that maybe it really wasn't Cindy who was killed. I thought, "Nobody who really knew Cindy ever saw her body. She had been identified by a dentist. But nobody we personally know actually saw her." I began daydreaming, "Maybe she'll still come back."

I went to one of the undertakers and asked, "Did you see Cindy?" He said, "Yes." Then I asked, "Did she still have her long blond hair?" He responded, "Yes, she did." I'm sure he was just trying to be helpful, but he was probably stretching the truth. It was a real tough time for me.

An important turning point came through a special women's seminar on prayer held at church a few weeks later. Also, the encouragement I received through the consistent prayer support and expressed concern of people was invaluable. It took several months, but eventually I got back on track.

I guess the kind of suffering we experienced is every parent's worst nightmare. There's no question about it—suffering forces us to trust in God. I had to get to the place where I genuinely believed and accepted that God did not make mistakes.

I can't say I've ever believed it was God's direct will that Cindy should be killed. But the facts are there are evil people in the world, and things do happen that we can't understand. There did come a point in my life when I had to decide to let God be God. I know that sounds a lot like a cliché, but it really did happen to me. I literally acknowledged that God is sovereign—and I had to leave it with that. With this kind of suffering, there's nothing else to do but to turn to God. Otherwise the bitterness will be self-destructive.

BILL: The suffering we've experienced has taught me to be thankful for what I do have. Cindy's older sister, Tammy, and her younger sister, Barbara, have been very close to us. We've always had a good relationship with the girls, but even more so from the moment their sister disappeared until now. I'm very thankful for our two daughters, our sons-in-law, and the grandchildren.

I'm also more thankful for my marriage. I believe our relationship has been strengthened because of what we've gone through. We have a solid marriage. Interestingly, I've read that the divorce rate among couples who have lost a child is much higher than the average. I guess that's because of all the accompanying stress, and blaming each other for what happened, and so forth. We've never blamed each other. Not once.

EDITH: I don't remember our marriage experiencing any significant stress because of Cindy's death. The situation was obviously stressful, but it drew us closer to each other, instead of driving us apart.

BILL: I'm also thankful for our good health, our friends, our church, our jobs. There are so many good things in our lives, and they've all come into focus more clearly because of the pain and suffering we've experienced as a family.

EDITH: Something I've learned that's very important: These kinds of tragedies can't be tied up in neat little packages. There are lots of dangling issues and unanswered questions that continue to linger. I'm trying not to overanalyze everything or even attempt to understand all of the whys.

Now this may make some folks a bit uncomfortable, but in response to all that's transpired since January 5, 1978, I can *not* honestly say, "Everything's just fine!" For example, both Bill and I feel some pain whenever we hear the song, "God Will Take Care of You." On the one hand, I know it's true; but there are times when I turn it off because, from my vantage point, God did not take care of Cindy. He really didn't. Sometimes I still struggle with that.

"How Can You Be Good?"

BILL: There's that chorus, "God Is So Good." Shortly after Cindy's disappearance, I remember the first time I sang that little chorus. I immediately questioned God and said, "How can You be good in taking our little daughter?" All of this is hard to reconcile, and it's impossible to try to explain logically. Occasionally, questions about God's goodness still come to mind—especially if I'm spiritually low. But in spite of what happened to Cindy, I choose to believe that God is good. The evil that happened is not a reflection on who God is.

Though, at times, a few church songs may be difficult for us, we've also experienced some healing through wonderful Christian music. One song, by Bill and Gloria Gaither, that really ministers to me—I think it was written around the time of our tragedy—says, "Joy comes in the morning. Hold on my child. The darkest hour is just before the dawn."

Getting on with life has been an adjustment for all of us in the family. Our youngest daughter, Barbara, has had her own unique set of issues to handle. When she was seventeen, she won a "Miss Teen" contest and went on to become Palm Beach County's "Junior Miss." Then, when newspaper articles were written up about her, some of them began by talking about Cindy. When she graduated from high school and went on to college at Taylor University years later, people would typically approach her with, "Tell us about Cindy." It's like she's constantly had to deal with it. Being Cindy's little sister has sort of shadowed her.

EDITH: We have experienced signs of healing through the years. Both of us think back on Cindy with great joy. For others, however, it's probably a bit awkward. I don't think they know whether they should talk to us about her or not. It's almost as if they need permission. Of course it's never pleasant to talk about the horrible things. But we take comfort in knowing that she's in heaven. So, when people take the initiative and relate incidents they experienced with Cindy, or talk about her personality or any specifics they knew about her—when people who loved her share with us on this level—that's always a delight.

BILL: Sometimes I'm concerned about whether people will remember Cindy. So it always helps whenever a person mentions her to us. It makes us realize that Cindy is still in people's thoughts. She's not been forgotten.

When I reflect on Cindy's life, I think it was short, but certainly not meaningless.

EDITH: I'm sure we'll never know the many ways her life and death have affected others. People may never tell us. But I know for some, their lives will never be the same. The few stories or books I've read about this sort of thing typically end with something wonderful taking place. Like at the funeral—scores of students turning their lives over to Christ—or whatever. Well, that didn't happen in our situation with Cindy.

In my own mind I occasionally wonder, "Did we handle this right? Did we take the opportunities to speak up? Or was there something lacking in our lives that these great things didn't happen? Might there have been more as a result of Cindy's death had we done something differently?" Questions like these still bother me somewhat.

On the other hand, Bill and I are very humbled when people talk about our faith. Our nephew, for instance, wrote an article about the impression we had made on him spiritually. A good friend shared in his Sunday School class about "the Redigers and their faith." Frankly, we've never felt worthy to be placed in the spotlight as if we're special. Actually we just sort of blundered our way through it all.

"She Named Her Cindy"

BILL: It was reported in a newspaper article that one of the detectives who worked on Cindy's case came to personal faith through the investigation. He attributed it to seeing that we had an inner strength he had never seen before. He was a veteran police officer at the peak of his career, in his mid-thirties, when he decided to retire from the force, uproot his family, and go to seminary to become a Baptist minister. He wanted to go into something where he could have a more positive influence on people's lives.

EDITH: Cindy had a friend in grade school who had become involved with the wrong crowd in high school. She got messed up in drugs. She dropped out of school. Cindy was very concerned about her. Several years after Cindy's death she contacted us to tell us she had become a Christian. She had a little girl, and she had named her Cindy.

She shared how she remembered Cindy singing to her when they were little girls, and Cindy directly asking her, "Are you a Christian?" This girl replied, "Well, no, my parents don't even go to church." Cindy told her, "All you have to do is open your heart and invite Jesus in." She told us she had never forgotten that. She said, "Cindy is directly responsible for my conversion."

BILL: Each year things get a little better. That first Christmas was especially difficult. But we've gone ahead and always tried to make the best of it. After all, we still have a family to enjoy and life to celebrate.

In fact, in recent years, three lovely granddaughters have come along to fill the void. It's thrilling to see life starting over—to see the process of life continuing on.

But still, there's rarely a day that goes by that I don't think of Cindy. Different things will bring her to mind. Every time I see a baton twirler, I envision her. Whenever I hear a band playing, she comes to mind. But now there's health and healing in those thoughts. I think of her positively these days.

❀ ❀ ❀

Significant Losses

I (Steve) don't think it's possible to read the Rediger's story without being reminded that life is precious, and truly fragile. There are no guarantees!

Only a few will ever face situations that parallel the intensity and horror of the murder of a child; and likely, fewer still, will handle it as gracefully and courageously as the Redigers. They are spiritual survivors. Even so, who of us can't relate to the heartache and heartbreak of some shattered hopes or broken dreams?

Sooner or later, all of us will experience major disappointments or significant losses. Perhaps you already have.

Special plans may have been carefully laid, expectations built up, specific action taken—but then, crash! Everything fell apart. You're devastated.

Or, all of a sudden, a spouse is gone. Perfectly healthy one moment, and then . . . gone. Death is always shocking. How will you be able to carry on all alone?

Or, without any warning, you find out that a loved one (or even yourself), has a terminal illness. It's as if—poof!—your future's shattered. Your dreams are in ashes.

Or, maybe your marriage isn't working. Though you vowed, "For better or worse" you never anticipated it would be lived out almost exclusively on the "worse" side.

Or, your shattered dreams may relate more to your business. It's struggling, definitely not flying! It was a great idea, had loads of potential, but just never got off the ground.

Perhaps you selected a career that was something you wanted to do as long as you can remember. You spent years and thousands of dollars educating yourself, but you never have been able to find a job in your field. Or maybe some doors opened for you, but you didn't have sufficient talent or expertise to make it work.

Possibly you've had a burden for a specific ministry. Deep within, for years you've longed to advance God's kingdom. But you've seen all your efforts dissolve in personality conflicts and nitpicky issues that were magnified to destructive proportions.

Your major disappointments might relate more to your children. They've made poor choices. They've refused the opportunities and input you've tried to give them. You've done the very best you knew how. Yet, they've rejected not only your values, but you as well.

Dreams in ashes. How they hurt!

When dreams are shattered, when crisis comes, when life is seemingly in ashes—what do we do? How do we survive?

Consider for a moment the Old Testament account of the life of Job. He was a respected, prosperous, God-fearing man who (according to Scripture) walked with the Lord and shunned evil. However, he suffered an incredible series of calamities. He lost his wealth, enemy invaders carried off his livestock and murdered his servants; and then, all ten of his children were killed when a storm came and the house where they were feasting collapsed on them.

In all of this tragedy, we're told that Job did not sin by blaming God. Job even lost his health; and while literally sitting in ashes, he said to his wife one day: "Shall we accept good from God, and not trouble?"

I marvel at Job. He amazes me! As he sat in the ashes of his life—ashes of broken dreams, incredible grief, pain, his business ruined, his family gone, in physical agony—in all of this he determined within his soul to trust God as the author of goodness. He set his heart toward the Lord. He allowed no negative thoughts about God to linger in his mind. He stood firm in his convictions, even in the face of disaffirmation from his wife and friends. "Curse God and die . . . confess your sins, whatever the monstrous deeds you've done to bring on these miseries," they told him.

To Job's credit, he remained faithfully steadfast in his crisis when there wasn't even a hint that God would bring beauty out of the ashes of his life.

Crisis—An Unwelcome Visitor

Crisis, in one form or another, is an unwelcome visitor, who eventually appears on all of our doorsteps. In fact, when Mr. Crisis comes, he just barges in! He never knocks, and his visits are always too long. His presence pollutes the atmosphere and never fails to add stress to family settings. He says things like: "Your life's out of control. Why don't you just give up? The worst is yet to come." And whenever Crisis—this unwanted guest—comes, we're forced to respond. For most, our response is typically anger, impatience, guilt, despair.

For the Christian, however, in beautiful contrast to the obnoxious, unwelcome presence of Mr. Crisis, concurrent with his visit (however long he stays), is another guest ready and available to enter into whatever situation any of us may face. But He (Christ) has manners and waits to be invited in.

He's always there, but unfortunately, too often He goes unnoticed. He's able to diffuse the tension Crisis creates. His presence reminds us to love and encourage one another . . . to be patient, gentle, kindhearted. He promises that He'll never forsake us. "I can make beauty out of these ashes," He says. "I'm still in control. Don't give up. Don't let your heart be troubled. I am with you. I won't pack my bags and leave just because painful, stress-filled, difficult times have come. Include Me!"

Bill and Edith Rediger have done just that. They've been honest about their agony and distress. Meanwhile, Christ has walked with them through all their pain and many adjustments—and still does!

Following one of our tennis matches about six years after Cindy's death, I remember asking Bill how he was *really* doing. He was completely honest. "Steve, it's very hard. I don't think I'll ever fully get over what happened. I still think about Cindy the last thing before I go to sleep, and first thing when I wake up. But we're going to make it because the Lord has helped us."

A while back, Valerie and I attended a Wheaton College production of Michael Brady's play *To Gillian on Her 37th Birthday*. The story line centered around the personal struggle of a grieving husband who had lost his wife two years earlier in a boating accident. At one point, a character in the play stated, "The people who experience great losses, either become kind . . . or go bad."

Though I'm not sure I can prooftext that statement with a specific Bible verse, it does capture a piece of reality. In the throes of our pain—our disappointments, our losses, our crisis—while sitting in the ashes of our burned-out dreams, each of us has a choice. We can lose heart, give up in despair, and become bitter; or, we can choose to trust the Lord who is with us. In other words, when the dreams of the righteous are shattered—when life is in ashes—we must choose to believe that the God who is with us is still working for our good. The key point being: We must choose to believe. Those are the exact words Bill Rediger used: "In spite of what happened to Cindy, I choose to believe that God is good.

The evil that happened is not a reflection on who God is."

The last thing I want to do is to trivialize or minimize the grief experienced when any of us suffers loss. When dreams are shattered, when crisis comes, there will always be emotional upheaval. And at that time people need space, and time, and tenderness, and understanding, and love. And most of all, what's needed is a sense of hope.

Paul affirmed this truth in Romans 8:28: "In all things God works for the good of those who love Him." When dreams are shattered, and the future is uncertain, we can find hope in choosing to believe that Christ has not forsaken us, but will eventually bring good out of the ashes of our lives.

What does this choice look like practically? It may sound good in theory, but how does it translate or connect to where each of us lives every day? Here's a suggestion I've learned from the Redigers: Believers must rehearse regularly the conviction that God is trustworthy. How? By beginning each day with a declaration like: "Lord, in You alone I find my security. Regardless of the events of this day, I'm choosing to acknowledge Your presence and believe You are actively working for my good."

We can also rehearse this conviction in conversation with others: "I don't know what the Lord has in mind; I don't know how He's going to do it; but I choose to trust God who can do all things—whose ultimate plans cannot be thwarted." Sound forced? Maybe even trite? Actually, those are words Job himself spoke: "Lord, I know that You can do all things; no plan of Yours can be thwarted" (Job 42:1-2). And as it turned out, at the end of Job's story, we read: "The Lord made him prosperous again and . . . blessed the latter part of Job's life more than the first" (42:10, 12). There it is: God made beauty from ashes!

When life is in ashes, in reality, we have only two options. Either God cares, or He doesn't care. From Job's life in Scripture, it's undeniably apparent that God *really does* care!

Last Will and Testament

In the February 1989 issue of *Reader's Digest,* there's a true life account of a young girl, Shari Smith, who was kidnapped and murdered the day before her high school graduation. Two days after her abduction the girl's murderer sent her parents a two-page letter captioned "Last Will and Testament." The article begins:

> Without a single word of self-pity, the teenager poured out her love for her family and words of faith: "I'll be with my Father now, so please don't worry! Don't ever let this ruin your lives, and keep living one day at a time for Jesus. My thoughts will always be with you." She closed with words evoking Paul's Epistle to the Romans: "Everything works out for the good of those that love God."

The faithfulness of this young girl facing a certain and sadistic death is almost unimaginable. Her murderer took her life, but he didn't snuff out her faith. Even in her death, Shari Smith was a spiritual survivor. And she's left behind some clues for the rest of us about enduring faith, even when all the physical evidence screams disbelief to our souls.

I'm confident, if Cindy could speak from heaven and say one thing to her parents and sisters and friends, like Shari Smith did, she'd say: "Please, don't ever let this ruin your lives. I'm with my Father. All is well with me." And furthermore, because Cindy is representative of so many others whose lives were cut short, I believe she would be joined by a chorus of children, ministering to their grieving loved ones: "Don't ever let this ruin your lives."

Best-selling author Rabbi Harold Kushner learned, when his first child, Aaron, was only three years old, that the boy had a rare disease. The illness would cause rapid aging, his hair would fall out, his growth would be stunted, and within a few years he would look like a little old man, and then die in his teens. Writing about this unjust, unacceptable death, he says: "I am a more sensitive person, a more effective pastor, a more sympathetic counselor because of Aaron's life and death than I would ever have been without it. And I would give up all of those gains in a second if I could have my son back. If I could choose, I would forego all the spiritual growth and depth which has come my way because of our experiences, and be what I was fifteen years ago, an average rabbi, an indifferent counselor, helping some people and unable to help others, and the father of a bright, happy boy. But I cannot choose."

I suspect, the Redigers would agree with Rabbi Kushner. They'd exchange having Cindy back for whatever "lessons learned" that resulted from their horrible ordeal. But the fact is, none of us will ever have those kinds of choices to make. Our choices are restricted to *how we respond* when major disappointments, significant losses, or crises come along. Old Testament Job, the Redigers, Shari Smith, and Rabbi Kushner have all chosen courageously. What an example they are! When the time comes—without a doubt—God will be pleased, and His purposes will be served, if you and I choose to do the same.

CHAPTER SEVEN
BACK FROM DESPAIR

Daryle Doden

If I have put my trust in gold or said to pure gold, "You are my security," if I have rejoiced over my great wealth . . . so that my heart was secretly enticed . . . then these also would be sins to be judged, for I would have been unfaithful to God on high.

Job 31:24-25, 27-28

Be still, and know that I am God.

Psalm 46:10

When you have nothing left but God, you begin to learn that God is enough.

Author Unknown

In all that God does with us, in all the puzzling vicissitudes of life, His purpose is the development of Christlike character, of pure selflessness, of agape love. Failure may be a better instrument to achieve that than success. If God is going to perfect Christlikeness in you and me, it may sometimes involve the failure of our ambitions, of our plans, of our dreams, of our hopes.

Paul Billheimer
The Mystery of His Providence

When I first met Daryle Doden, I (Steve) was just a high school junior. My sister, Brenda, brought him home from Moody Bible Institute, where they were both students, wanting my parents to meet the new "friend" in her life. During that visit it wasn't long before he mentioned that they wanted to get married! (I wasn't even aware she had broken up with her previous boyfriend, whom I knew fairly well and really liked.)

Having a great deal of respect for my sister, however, I was willing to be open-minded. It didn't take long to notice that Daryle was opinionated and had no trouble expressing himself. I wasn't always certain how to process everything he said. He had very definite ideas and knew where he stood on most issues. At times I found that a bit intimidating. Brenda said, when she first met him, she was especially attracted to his strong leadership qualities.

After graduating from high school and enrolling at Moody Bible Institute, I had an opportunity to get to know Daryle a lot better. By this time Daryle was in his senior year and officially engaged to my sister. In fact, we played together on the school's basketball team for one season.

Daryle has always been a fascinating personality. I'm continually amazed at his wide variety of interests and the multiple areas of expertise he's developed. Daryle is a visionary, a self-starter, and exceptionally bright. My sister knew that long ago. It's become more obvious to the rest of us with the passing of time.

Over these past twenty-five years, Valerie and I have grown to appreciate, love, and respect Daryle immensely. We've often remarked, "There are few people we know who have demonstrated more noticeable change and spiritual maturity than Daryle Doden." His capacity for growth has been phenomenal! His personal integrity, spiritual convictions, and increasing compassion and care for others have all had a far-reaching impact for Christ and His kingdom. I believe that will only continue more significantly in the days ahead.

Daryle Doden is the president of Ambassador Steel Corporation, headquartered out of Auburn, Indiana. He founded the company by selling steel from a pay phone. Early in 1974, he incorporated with a sales volume of $50,000 during the first month. Annual sales are now in excess of 80 million dollars. He's the father of five, and presently he serves on nationally-known ministry boards. For years he's taught an adult Sunday School class at his church, serves as a lay counselor, and travels regularly to speak or consult for churches and for select groups of businesspeople.

Daryle Doden's personal journey has been far from easy, but he has persisted courageously and stubbornly. I believe his honesty will grab your heart. And I'm certain each of us will identify with parts of his story. He's another breed of spiritual survivor.

❀ ❀ ❀

"Financially Poor"

I was brought up in a very modest home. Actually, we were poor in terms of financial resources, though there was a lot of love and respect, which we demonstrated for one another within our family. My father, a fundamentalist Baptist pastor, was a strong man of faith. It was a humble, simple faith, but he lived out at home what he preached in the pulpit. I think the most money Dad ever made in one week was about $85, not including the benefits of living in a parsonage. Somehow, my folks scratched out a living and managed to get by. We never had much materially, but my older sister and I knew our parents really loved us. My dad, sixteen years older than Mom, died eleven years ago at the age of seventy-four. I was thirty-four at the time.

In my youth my folks instilled within me the importance of always doing what's right regardless of how popular or unpopular it might be. I was encouraged to stand up for what I believed and to have opinions about anything and everything—provided I could support them biblically. This kind of upbringing forced me to become an independent thinker and gave me a strong sense of self. Years later I came to realize that my "opinionated approach" toward life was often perceived by others as arrogance, which wasn't necessarily an endearing quality.

For as long as I can remember, I had assumed that I would be successful at whatever I attempted to do. I believed in who I was. Wanting to follow in Dad's footsteps, I had always thought my success would be experienced in ministry, not in business. But interestingly, the way I got into business was the result of failure in ministry. In my early years of marriage, I served two different churches, but because of relational conflicts and other circumstances the jobs just never worked out—so in my mind, I had failed.

I had anticipated success, but never in the business world. When that happened, I was probably more surprised than anybody else. In fact, those early years in business were almost like living in Disneyland—too good to be true. When I first started, within a matter of months, I went from $100 a week, to $200 a week, to $600 a week—and then, we thought we had arrived in Fantasyland!

Actually, my company, Ambassador Steel Corporation, was born out of being jobless. I had just left a church and needed to put food on the table for my family—my wife and three small children. Learning that the steel used to reinforce concrete (commonly called "rebar") was in short supply, I contacted a friend in the steel business and asked him whether he had some rebar I could sell. He said he did. So I went to a pay phone in a nearby mall (to avoid long distance charges!), and, after a couple hours of calling around, I sold the steel. I found it surprisingly easy. The profits from that one day were more money than I had ever made in any previous month of my life! As a result, my friend said, "Obviously you have some real abilities in this area. Maybe we ought to start a business."

Subsequently, a few of us got together and scraped up some starting capital (a grand total of $2,000), and Ambassador Steel Corporation was born. Most people are more familiar with the product we deal in than they might realize. For example, when new highways are constructed (or reconstructed), you'll typically see long and bent pieces of steel rod—usually with a green tint—embedded in the concrete of the roadway being built. That's the reinforcing bar or "rebar" that we buy and sell. Since that rather humble beginning back in late 1973 (we incorporated in 1974), we've grown to be one of the largest distributors and fabricators of reinforcing bar in the Midwest.

By nature, I'm a goal-oriented, principle-driven person. And I bought into a very simple philosophy. Live by certain principles and achieve predictable results. As a believer, that meant to me: Obey God's guidelines, and He will bless you. It was like a formula for success. Biblical principles, plus (+) obedience, plus (+) consistency, equals (=) success. In my mind it was all spelled out in Scripture. How could it be more clear?

I even developed a testimony that I gave to men's groups across the country. As the business continued to prosper, it gave me more and more opportunities to share my formula for success. In essence my message was: "If you faithfully follow God's principles, you will experience success in life—like I have. Therefore, if you are not experiencing success, then obviously you are violating some biblical principle or principles. You need to face your problems head on—figure out what you're overlooking, make adjustments, and then get on with it!" Actually (it's kind of embarrassing to admit this), I became an expert at trying to "fix" other people.

Like a lot of successful people, down deep I had thought my success was really attributed to me—as if I were someone uniquely special. Too often those who experience success fail to realize (if I can put it in this way), the luck of the draw. The truth is, there are a number of factors that contribute to anyone's success—having a marketable idea, being well-connected, the matter of timing, the support of others, and of course, the sovereignty of God, to mention a few. Unknowingly, I had fallen into erroneous thinking, believing I was the main reason for my success. I had subconsciously become overconfident, even oversecure. Inadvertently, I had moved from confidence to cockiness.

In 1981, after experiencing remarkable success in business for seven consecutive years, I began focusing my energies and attention in some other areas. Over the next four years I became less and less involved in the day-by-day operations of Ambassador Steel and was giving myself almost exclusively to other time-consuming projects—a couple of them related to my church. Whenever an appealing business deal would come along, however, I'd jump back in and get involved. For example, during these years, one huge contract I put together was furnishing over 10,000 tons of rebar (from a canceled nuclear project) to Red China. That's the equivalent of an entire trainload of over 110 cars full of steel. Pulling off this deal involved approximately seven months, a lot of travel, and loads of pressure—though it was the sort of thing I thrived on. There's nothing like the thrill of cutting a deal!

"Takeovers"

I went immediately from that experience into pursuing a takeover of a potentially profitable company that was just lying dormant—and this was before "takeovers" became so fashionable in the business world. At that time it was kind of a cutting-edge thing to do. Right on the heels of that, my wife, Brenda, and I started building our dream house. And frankly—though I wouldn't admit it then—it was a house that was far beyond our means. It required the ongoing success and growth of our business just to complete it. Without understanding it, or taking the time to stop and evaluate what was happening, all of these activities were creating a huge amount of stress in my life.

I had begun to develop an uneasy feeling that the tremendous success I was experiencing could not last indefinitely. I was thinking more and more that we did not deserve this "dream world" we were living in. It was kind of a sooner or later the-other-shoe-is-going-to-have-to-drop mentality. Thus, in the back of my mind there was growing apprehension, a premonition, that something bad was going to happen. Then, in January of 1985, I received a phone call from a trusted business associate in Texas. When I received the call, I just had a sixth sense that it would be the realization of that dreaded premonition. And I was right.

My associate reported that one of our key employees, who managed our Texas operations, had not shown up for work. Without any warning he had simply disappeared. When I heard that news, I was immediately convinced that something was terribly wrong. As we began uncovering a few facts in the wake of his disappearance, it became apparent that he had been involved in a secret lifestyle. We also learned that he had embezzled about $35,000 from our company. That angered me, but we could afford to absorb the loss. The most significant damage, however, was he had made some business deals that were potentially ruinous to our corporation. Upon investigating all the legal ramifications, it became clear that his verbal commitments regarding a number of major transactions were legally binding and enforceable because—by virtue of his position and the authority we had entrusted to him—he was speaking for the corporation.

I was devastated. All along I was aware that I had violated some important principles in hiring this man. I knew in advance he had a checkered past. Initially, I had some strong intuitive feelings about not bringing him into our company, but with the encouragement of my partner I quelled those feelings in search of big profits. Even though I wasn't enthusiastic about it, we gave him the benefit of the doubt, hoping that his past was really behind him. We brought him into the corporation (against my better judgment), not so much because of pressure from my partner, but because of the profit motive. Therefore, I agreed to hire him.

Immediately I began to blame myself. I couldn't accuse anybody else for what had happened—not my partner, not even the dishonest employee—because I was the one who allowed that man to have the power to make those decisions. That was the hardest thing for me, a principle-driven person, to deal with. Later, while I received counseling, the phrase I used was: "I did it to myself." There was nobody to blame, but me!

Another matter that was troubling me at the time was the house we were building. We had overdreamed, overbuilt, and now with it only partially finished—the brick structured shell was standing and roofed (all 12,000 square feet of it, not including the three-car garage and the detached three-car carriage house)—it became very apparent that we were in way over our heads. Again, there was no one else I could blame for my predicament but me. I was like that man Jesus referred to (in a parable in Luke 14) who didn't sit down long enough to estimate accurately how much it would cost him to build. I had not fully counted the cost. How could I have been so foolish! I envisioned myself becoming a laughing stock in the community because, by then, I had concluded that the house would never be completed. It was as if, unwittingly, I was going to have a living monument of my own violation of God's principles.

That phone call from Texas was like the lever that opened the floodgates. All at once these overwhelming thoughts and fears about the future came rushing in. And with my simplistic approach to life, I had developed no coping mechanisms to deal with what was happening to me. All of a sudden, life seemed out of control.

"Big-Time Failure"

I couldn't get over the sense that I was failing big time. Here I was "the successful businessman" who had taken a strong stand for Christ and biblical principles. I had preached passionately, "Trust God . . . keep His principles . . . and you'll be successful . . . like me!" To fail, I concluded, would not only be personally humiliating, but also bring great discredit to the Lord.

I developed all kinds of paranoias and jumped to irrational conclusions almost instantly. I was caught up in a vortex of fears. I was afraid I would lose everybody's respect—including my family's. I was fearful about the loss of all of my financial resources. Then I questioned my ability to hold down another job. I imagined I would never be in a position to afford to send any of my five children to college. I thought we were going to have to prepare for poverty. It was very much a "bunker mentality." And I felt stuck!

I was absolutely convinced that we were going to be totally ruined with no visible means of recovering. In my mind, we were facing certain bankruptcy. (However, all of this was projection on my part, prompted by one telephone call and a lot of assumptions. I was not taking a realistic look at all of the facts.)

Over the next six weeks I began to deteriorate physically. I couldn't sleep. I had never experienced that before. I've always been a person who falls asleep a couple of minutes after my head hits the pillow. I didn't know how to deal with that. I lost weight. My stomach felt as though there was ice churning inside. All kinds of wild thoughts were racing through my mind. It was as though I was on an adrenaline high. All my waking hours I vacillated between "fight or flight." And I was definitely leaning toward flight!

I had never before heard the phrase, *clinical depression.* I had heard of *stress burnout,* and I always assumed that an executive-type person (like me) suffering from that would take a personal retreat for a few days—maybe a week—play several rounds of golf, and get over it. No big deal! So I didn't immediately seek outside help. Within three or four weeks, however, I was in very bad shape emotionally.

I was not comfortable talking with very many people about what I was experiencing. In Christian circles, probably most of us sense (a certain amount of) pressure to be upbeat. At least I did. I didn't want to say much about what I was really feeling. But I was completely honest with my wife.

None of our five children knew specifically what was happening in Dad's life for some time. It was probably seven or eight weeks before we finally said something to them. Until then, the older children (in their early teens) were only confused and anxious. They knew something was going on, but they didn't have a clue what it was. The only thing they knew for sure was that Mom and Dad were spending an awful lot of time upstairs in their room talking. We eventually learned that all along they were thinking that Brenda and I were having some major marital problems. It was actually a great relief to them to find out that their parents were not getting a divorce. Dad was just sick!

Later my oldest son, Eric, who tends to be extremely sensitive—sometimes even fearful—said to Brenda, "Mom, Dad's never going to get well, is he?"

"Not Dealing with Reality"

I had made myself literally sick, based on the fear of what *might* happen. It was strictly projection. I was not dealing with reality. My partner and associates would say to me, "Daryle, things are not that bad. The bank will still work with us." But I would not listen to them. Because I was convinced that nobody understood as well as I did how much money we were really going to lose because of the bad decisions and multiple transactions we were committed to in Texas.

I could not let go of how dumb I had been. I had violated my principles. It was all my fault! I let it happen by not being involved enough in the day-by-day operations. I felt I had failed my partner and the entire company. I would not let myself off the hook. The negative self-talk and fears just multiplied and dominated my mind continually.

I didn't try to get help for myself because I believed my situation was totally hopeless. My attitude was, "Whatever bad happens, I have it coming . . . I deserve to be sick . . . besides, there's nothing anybody could do that would really help . . . the problems are too big and irreversible." The mental anguish was as real to me as if all of my projections had actually occurred.

I was stressed out, becoming seriously depressed, and I was beginning to self-destruct because of my rigid belief system and simplistic philosophy of life. It was a "live by the sword, die by the sword" mentality. My outlook, "live by certain principles and achieve predictable results," was about to do me in. I felt I had lost God's blessing because I had violated His principles by choosing to ignore all the warning signals when hiring the man in Texas with the checkered past. Emotionally, I was falling into a bottomless pit.

I was on a downward spiral going deeper and deeper. It was getting darker, and the question that haunted me was, "Are the Everlasting Arms ever going to catch *me?*" It's not that I questioned whether God existed in the general sense, but did He exist for me? Up to this point in my life, my faith had been pretty academic and not very relational. Experientially, I had no means of knowing whether I was really going to be caught, or whether I would just fall onto the rocks of life and be shattered. Furthermore, I was convinced I did not deserve to be caught. In my head I was thinking, "If ultimately I'm going to be shattered anyway, why not just shortcut the process and end it all myself."

However, looking back on that horrible, unstable, lonely journey into despair, I can now say that there were some positive things beginning to happen to me. For the first time in my "principled life," I looked around and noticed that there were all kinds of godly people I had never accounted for who were going through very difficult experiences. I thought of solid Christian businesspeople who had experienced financial disaster. I thought of people who had lost children as a result of tragedy. Then there were other wonderful Christians who, without any warning, suddenly lost a spouse. In other countries people were in prison for serving Jesus. I could see no principle that any of these folks had broken, and yet they suffered.

I also began to realize that I had never really dealt with my insecurities about personal relationships. I had an inferiority complex. And I might clear something up here. I see a vast difference between low self-esteem and an inferiority complex. Low self-esteem, as I view it, implies that a person feels poorly, or a sense of shame, about who he or she is. Whereas, I think of an inferiority complex as referring to someone's reticence toward others because of a perception that people feel negatively about him or her.

I never had a problem with low self-esteem. I felt very good about myself. I always believed I could achieve and be successful. But I suspected and assumed that others felt I did not deserve to succeed. I never perceived that people thought of me as a good guy or saw me as someone who was smart or had a lot to offer. I had this sense that there was something unlikable about me, but I wasn't exactly sure what it was. And so, part of my personality, or drive to succeed, was to prove continually to everybody that I really was who *I thought* I was. It was terribly important in my mind that no one could ever look at me and say, "Yeah, I knew it all along that his success in life was just a temporary fluke!"

"I Felt So Dead Inside"

In spite of these new-to-me thoughts, or insights, I continued on a downward spiral into a deeper depression. Increasingly suicide seemed like a viable option. Just trying to function became more difficult with every passing day. It was almost impossible for me to stand up in the church choir any longer and try to sing the praises of God when I felt so dead inside. From my vantage point, life was pretty much over.

People in our church were becoming somewhat aware that all was not well with me, but because most thought I was just physically sick, they didn't ask many questions. I was pretty good at "faking it" in public. However, I began to develop what counselors call the mask of depression—an almost unexplainable, but very real look—slumped shoulders, kind of a hang-dog expression.

By this time it was the end of February and only six weeks since that phone call that began this whole process in me. It had all happened pretty fast.

I've always been very verbal. During these weeks I shared in detail all of my feelings of insecurity with my wife, Brenda. Initially it was difficult on her. It made her fearful because the person she trusted and counted on was, all of a sudden, uncharacteristically wobbly. And then, when I started talking about ending my life so she could collect on an insurance policy in order to live "happily ever after" without a drag like me around . . . well, she rose to the occasion.

During this period of time, her faith only increased. She was convinced that in some fashion, God was going to see us through. Meanwhile, I would do my best to break down that faith. On the one hand, I really did not want her to enter into my despair, but at the same time, I tried to do all I could to make her as discouraged as I was because I wanted her to see my point and agree with my sick logic.

But she was unyielding! God gave her incredible strength. Since she had just had surgery for carpal tunnel syndrome on both of her wrists, she was unable to do anything else except deal with me and all of my problems.

Prior to this time in my life, I had never experienced stress in the way most people speak of it. In fact, I did not even know there was such a thing as anxiety attacks. Here I was experiencing them, but did not understand what they were. The ice in the pit of my stomach was there, but I had no idea what it was. I now realize the phenomenon was actually adrenaline flowing through my system warning me of danger. But I just wrote off all the physical symptoms happening to my body as emotional or spiritual depression. And I thought it was a causative depression. Again, it was a simple formula: If I could just remove the cause, my depression would be gone. But, since I was the cause—my life was out of control, and in my mind failure was certain, and nothing was going to change that—I concluded that I was without hope. It was obvious. Life, for me, was over.

It became clear that the best thing that could possibly come out of all of this would be if I could just die. Then my family would inherit some insurance money, making sure the children could go to college and have the things they deserve. I prayed that the Lord would take my life. I also prayed that somehow God would destroy that partially built "dream house" so there would be more insurance benefits to collect. And then, of course, once I started praying for death, I began to think of ways I could help God along. As I said, my mind was racing wildly with all kinds of bizarre and irrational thoughts.

Fortunately at that time, God brought back into our lives some longtime friends, Steve and Maria Gardner. They had heard through the grapevine that "Daryle and Brenda are not doing well," but even the people who told them did not know why. They sensed, however, that something was terribly wrong. As I look back on what God was doing through these friends, the whole scenario was amazing. God was at work in His timing to accomplish His purposes. There I was, a person more committed to principles than to people, which on a practical level meant personal relationships were not very significant to me. And yet, here were these friends who cared enough and loved me enough to try to interfere in my life and really help!

The day they called was an all new low point for me. It was the first morning that I couldn't force myself out of bed. I had pulled the covers over my head and said to myself, "I'm just not going to get up today. I can't function anymore."

It was very late in the morning when our phone rang.

Steve and Maria didn't ask. They just announced that they were coming over. That meant I had to get up! When they arrived, I was still in my pajamas. So I put on my bathrobe. Maria, who herself has dealt with some personal emotional issues, didn't waste any time. Without mincing words, she went right to the heart of the matter and asked, "Daryle, have you contemplated suicide?"

I had to be honest. I admitted that I saw it as my only viable option. Then she said something that burned into my conscience. I'll never forget it. "Daryle," she said, "you realize that suicide breeds suicide!" As a lay counselor myself, I immediately understood what she meant. In other words, if one member of a family, particularly the father, who is a major influence on the children, takes his own life, then very possibly one of his children may eventually take the same escape route.

I loved my kids dearly. And instantly I knew I could not even crack the door open to that terrible possibility in their lives. I could not do that to my children, or my wife. Maria's directness made me face the harsh realities of what I had been considering. As a result of that brief encounter, suicide ceased to be an option in my mind—though I did not share that decision with Brenda or anybody else.

Now I was in a real dilemma. There was no way out! My anxiety level only increased. My body sprung into high gear. I could not sit still, or sleep. I'd jump out of bed in the middle of the night, run over to the trampoline, and then run in place for at least five minutes. I didn't understand what was happening to me. (Again, I was unaware that it was the result of adrenaline rushing through my system.) I had all these weird feelings and physical symptoms for which I had no explanation. What had started out as an emotional response to a business decision (to which I overreacted and was completely irrational), had become a serious spiritual problem, and now it had turned into a very real physical problem. I was a mess!

By now, word was getting out that Daryle Doden was really struggling. And unfortunately, the tendency of some of the people in my life, who meant so well, was to be like Job's friends. Let me explain. First, I have a very high view of Job's friends in the Old Testament. They came from a long distance to be with him. And, when they saw Job, they were very sensitive and put on the appropriate clothes of weeping and mourning for him. They even sat with him for seven days just to experience his pain. But then, they made the same mistake that most of us make. They wanted to "fix it" for him. They tried to give him answers. But none of their answers would suffice. Eventually, God Himself encountered Job and declared, "Where were you when I laid the earth's foundation? Tell Me, if you understand. Who marked off its dimensions? Surely you know! Who stretched a measuring line across it?" . . . and on and on God cross-examined him. I think God went to great lengths to make a point: "Listen, *you* don't have the answers. You don't have the capacity to figure out what's going on. Trust Me!"

"Finding 'the Answers' "

Likewise, some of my well-meaning friends, who cared for me deeply, were trying to give me answers or solutions to what I was experiencing. What I've come to understand is, when going through intense personal struggle or pain, what's really needed is someone willing to come alongside, and just be there. Finding "the answers" isn't necessarily helpful. In fact, often, circumstances may be such that answers can't even be processed for a time. What's really needed when facing crisis is hand-holding, and encouragement, and knowing that people care. Then perhaps, eventually, God will reveal His purposes—in His time. But maybe not. He alone will decide.

The next sequence of events I experienced came about as a result of my pastor's concern. He understood a little bit about clinical depression, and he really encouraged me to go to a hospital for some help. However, I was convinced and very fearful that, if I went to a hospital, and if word got out about my condition, the bank would immediately withdraw our line of credit, and that would be the death knell to our business. It was full-blown paranoia on my part.

I was so desperate for help, however, that I finally agreed to go to an out-of-state hospital. Once I arrived, it soon became obvious to me that the hospital wasn't set up to deal with much more than normal worker's stress. In addition, I was not very cooperative. When they administered the psychological testing, I understood well enough the answers they were looking for, thus, I just gave the responses needed that would help me bluff my way out. The diagnosis came back that I was mildly depressed. Within three days, I was released.

While in the hospital, they put me on a mild antidepressant drug. It helped me sleep a little. Physically, however, my bodily systems were so off balance that it didn't seem to make much difference. I continued to deteriorate in the weeks that followed throughout the month of March. I was feeling more and more desperate. I started looking for another job. I still had a job, but I wasn't even functioning in it. I was looking for anything. In fact, I actually talked to one of my employees about the possibility of moving my entire family into his home—all seven of us! And God bless him, his family was open to it.

A few weeks later, Brenda's parents were visiting us for the weekend. It was the third Sunday in April. The business had already begun to turn around. We were actually recovering from the Texas fiasco. But, in my state of mind, that wasn't helping me a bit.

All of us went to the Sunday evening church service. For me, church had become my only haven. I had never gone through a time of questioning who God was. But now I was going through the process of questioning whether the God I had spent a lifetime learning about actually existed. I seriously wondered whether there was someone out there who would really hear my despairing cry. In spite of all these disjointed throughts, however, I still loved going to church because I could turn off my mind for a while and feel safe. I knew, for at least the next hour, nothing more could happen to me.

Nevertheless, on this particular Sunday night, while the service was in process, I just couldn't sit any longer. It was as though jumping beans were on the loose inside my stomach. So I got up out of the pew, slipped out of the sanctuary, and went outdoors, hoping to walk off some of the racing energy I felt internally. (Fleeting thoughts of suicide still occasionally haunted me, even though I had already settled it in my mind that it was no longer an option.) As I began walking, I passed by the twenty-five-acre pond on our church campus. I remember thinking how wonderful it would be to jump into that pond, let the waves roll over me, and sink into oblivion. I was still walking around outside, thinking those kinds of thoughts, when the service ended. My wife panicked when she couldn't find me right away. She feared that perhaps I had thrown myself into the pond.

There were a number of people walking the grounds searching for me, including both of my parents-in-law. As God would have it, my father-in-law, whom I admire and love dearly, and my pastor found me. My father-in-law is a caring man, but not very demonstrative about his feelings. As the three of us were walking back toward the church building, I noticed tears in his eyes. He turned to my pastor and said, "We love this boy. We want to help him." It was the first time I'd ever heard that from him. And though he didn't say it directly to me, it didn't matter. His words ministered powerfully to my wounded spirit. I knew then that I was really loved, even though I didn't always feel loved. In fact, that incident was a major turning point. It made me willing to seek professional help. Though I was still convinced no one could help, at least, now I was willing to try.

I went for an initial interview with a godly Christian psychiatrist. Afterward he told my wife that, if I would not willingly cooperate and agree to be hospitalized, she should get the assistance of her parents and two brothers to have me committed. At first, I was willing. When the day came for me to check in, however, as soon as we got into the car I had second thoughts. Brenda literally had to physically wrestle me to get me to the preadmittance interview. That was the beginning of a real trauma experience.

As a hospital psychiatrist was interviewing me, I was thinking to myself, "If I do a pretty good job convincing this guy I don't have any problems, I won't even be admitted." At the conclusion of the interview the doctor said, "Daryle, it's very clear to me that you need to be checked in immediately for an extended period."

I was flabbergasted. "What do you mean?" I asked.

"Look," he said. "For an hour and a half, you have clearly and articulately told me your whole situation in such rapid-fire fashion that I can guarantee your adrenaline flow is wide open. You have the physiological symptoms of clinical depression."

I was still in denial at that point. "Well," I said, "if you could change the cause, I'd be OK. But you can't change the cause."

"You're right," he responded. "I can't change the cause. But we can help you cope with the issues you're facing. And, in order to do that we need you to get physically strong, as well as spiritually strong. That will be our goal here."

The fact of the matter was, I had been on supercharge from the middle of January, and now it was the end of April. The mounting internal stress level had opened my adrenaline flow to the point that my personal resources were depleted. I was physically exhausted and completely spent emotionally and spiritually.

Fortunately, there are a number of miracle drugs that have been developed to help overcome this physiological problem. Of course, they don't solve spiritual problems, or emotional problems. They do, however, play a very important part in the healing process. At first, it was a struggle for me to humble myself and submit to taking these medications; but now, I thank the Lord that these miracle drugs exist. They stopped the adrenaline flow.

During the first two weeks in the hospital, I detected no significant change in my mental state. I did, however, almost immediately begin to sleep better. (I know my wife did as well, without having me at home to cope with.) I could sense that I was getting stronger physically.

God has created all of us so marvelously! I've been told the body will repair itself from a clinical depression between six months to two years, assuming appropriate rest and food are provided. In fact, with proper medication, it's possible to accelerate the physical healing process to a three- to six-month period, allowing a person to deal more quickly and effectively with the real issues.

"Making Major Decisions"

Frequently, when a person is in the grips of a deep depressive state like the one I was in, he or she may do something drastic—make a foolish financial decision, get a divorce, commit suicide, or do some other irrational thing. The point is: No one should ever make any major decisions about life while experiencing severe depression.

For me, just being in a mental hospital was, in and of itself, a major stress factor. There was a huge gap between what I anticipated and what the reality was. I was expecting more of an executive retreat-center atmosphere. That's the impression I had from the way it was presented to me. I was assured that I could stay dressed in my street clothes, and that there would be lots of activities and, of course, good meals. In my head, I was thinking golfing, time to read, opportunity to relax, and so on. But at the time I was admitted, it just so happened that I was the only professional there for treatment. A number of the patients were on welfare. My roommate was a prison guard who had freaked out when someone threw human excrement on him. In addition, there were a lot of heavy smokers, and other patients were continually using foul language. It was a very uncomfortable environment for me!

What a predicament! There I was, a nonrelational person surrounded by people I had nothing in common with. It took me two weeks before I gave in and started relating to the other patients. A few of them shared with me that, at first, they thought I was a staff plant because I could articulate the psychological terms and would intellectualize my problems. But the fact is, that's just the way I'm wired. I've got to verbalize out loud to process what's happening.

The hospital experience was in many ways extremely stressful. Yet, while I was there, I started reading a book someone had given me, titled *Depression: Finding Hope and Meaning in Life's Darkest Shadow.* The coauthor, Don Baker, is a highly successful pastor who experienced a deep depression far more severe than mine in both its length and ramifications. I identified very much with what he went through. His depression was four years in duration. And while he was still pastoring, he checked himself into a hospital for six months.

In his book he shares about the humiliation of going into the hospital. He talks about walking through the entrance and noticing that one of the receiving nurses was a young gal from his church. "She greeted him with disbelief flashing across her face. 'Pastor,' she said, 'what are you doing . . .' and her voice trailed off into nothingness as awareness finally displaced her confusion."

Later he writes: "It was a wise and insightful counselor who . . . gently said, 'I'm sure, Mr. Baker, that the doctor's original diagnosis is correct. You are deeply depressed—you do need help—you do need to be here—but you'll get better. It will take time, but you'll get better.' "

About that particular incident Don Baker writes: "For four years I had been clinging to the slippery sides of that deep, black hole: sometimes falling, then recovering; then falling and again recovering until finally I could hold on no longer. I had plummeted into the deepest recesses of that impenetrable darkness. But even as the darkness lingered and deepened, there was now one faint glimmer of light flipped on by a wise and gentle counselor whose name has long since been forgotten. 'You'll get better—it may take time, but you'll get better.' "

When I read that part of the book, the thought occurred to me, "If Don Baker got better, maybe I could get better too." That was truly the first glimmer of hope I had sensed in over three months—from mid-January to the fourth week of April. It was a tiny ray of light in my dark experience.

I appreciated the book immensely. The first half is about Don Baker's experience. Coauthor Emery Nester, a personal friend of Don's wrote the second half. Interestingly, Emery is a psychologist, who was unable to "fix" his friend. None of his professional training, none of his previous pastoral experience, nothing he was able to do could make things right for Pastor Baker. Indeed, all Emery ends up doing is walking through Don's experience with him. What a powerful lesson that was for me! Even though Emery Nester could not "fix" Don Baker, he could still walk with his friend through the darkness.

My journey back to normality has been a process. I was hospitalized for three weeks. Looking back, I should have stayed in much longer. I had a very difficult first week back. I was unable to go to the office. However, by the end of June, I was probably functioning at about 50 percent capacity. My family, business associates, friends, and my church were all very supportive and patient with me. An important part of my healing was learning to focus on facts—what's real, and concentrating on one day at a time. As the weeks and months have passed, I gradually felt stronger, and healthier, and eventually got back on track. After about a year I was probably 95 percent whole. For a long time I thought I'd never get back beyond 95 percent. And, in a way, I didn't want to. I did not want to lose my new sensitivity to people who were hurting.

Today (seven years later) I'm fully functioning again; though frankly, I'm still processing my experience with depression. As it turned out, our business did not fail. In fact, it has flourished! Earlier this year, we finally completed the last room in our home. (The house project took eight years to finish.)

"Guilt"

There's a part of me that almost feels guilty for not having failed. I was in the trenches with all the hurting people; and there are still millions of folks (Christians and non-Christians) who are deeply hurting in this world. Yet, how is it that God has been so good to me? I have such a terrific wife and five beautiful kids. I am so blessed. My life is wonderful. God's grace toward me is abundant and beyond explanation.

In some ways I feel like a person who has faced death and survived—and now, no longer fears death. There's a part of me that believes I've faced my worst fears. Even though they never materialized, I faced them just the same. During my depression they were as real to me as if they had actually occurred. But I have survived. And even though the future is uncertain, and there are no guarantees, I am not nearly as fearful about failure or some of the other possibilities as I was before my journey into despair.

Did the Everlasting Arms catch me? It depends on how I choose to interpret what happened. If I interpret that to mean that God prevented me from hurting myself on the rocks . . . then, maybe He didn't. The truth is, no one is immune from experiencing life with its accompanying struggles and certain trauma. Even believers are not necessarily saved from pain. But will God always be there? Yes. Absolutely! I have a renewed sense of the reality of God's presence in my life.

During my intense period of crisis, I was never angry at God. I was angry at myself. Prior to January of 1985, I had always been hard on other people who didn't "tough it out" when problems came along. I saw them as weak and unprincipled, sometimes even unspiritual. Essentially, my "compassion tank" was on empty. Through this experience I saw myself—perhaps for the first time—as a sinner in need of God's grace. I had been a Christian as long as I could remember, but I never had an accurate view of how loathsome my judgmental spirit and sinfulness really was. And yet, I also had to be willing to accept God's forgiveness. For a period of time I just couldn't do that.

God has created within me a new sensitivity, a new compassion for others. Probably more than anything else, I've come to realize, and now believe, that people are more important than principles and procedures—and also, that relationships matter more than rules or rituals. Of course, that doesn't mean I should violate rules, but they dare not become the focal point of my life. My relationship with God and with others must be primary and foremost. Otherwise I'm missing the whole message of Jesus: "To love God with all my heart, soul, mind, and strength—and my neighbor as myself." This continues to be my personal growth edge.

"I Will Trust You"

During my time of despair in the hospital, the Book of Job became a very warm, meaningful section of Scripture to me.

And it remains that to this day. I literally came to the point in my own crisis where I echoed Job's words: "Even if You slay me, I will trust You." I settled it once and for all: "God, I believe in You . . . I believe You exist . . . I believe You are sovereign . . . I believe because I *choose* to believe."

I remember looking up at the sky, as I was walking around the hospital grounds, and having a tremendous sense of how small I am—and how fragile life is. We all have a tendency to think that our daily routine and our particular circumstances are very important. In light of eternity, however, present-day schedules and specific concerns are pretty insignificant. I agree with Job, God doesn't have to answer to me. And that's where I am today.

Even so, there are still many times when I don't understand the way God operates. I'd prefer that everybody had a happy family and enough money to meet their needs. But I don't allow myself to dwell on those concerns. I immediately turn such thoughts over to God. It's not up to me to approve or disapprove of what He allows to happen or chooses to do.

I'm in the process of becoming a liberated person. I now think of my life as A.S. (after sickness), rather than as B.S. (before sickness). As an A.S., I've come to realize and accept that there is no security in business. There is no such phenomenon as financial security. I presently view the Ambassador Steel Corporation as more than merely *my* business. There are 150 people who work for this company, and I have to think in terms of what's beneficial for all of these people—not just what benefits Daryle Doden. I didn't have that perspective before as a B.S. I currently think of myself as the custodian of certain assets that have to mutually benefit all who are involved.

As a businessman (A.S.), I'm also much more "win-win" in my approach to making deals. From the very beginning I look for what will benefit my suppliers as well as what will be advantageous to Ambassador, whereas before (B.S.), I'd be protective of Ambassador and let the rest of the chips fall wherever. For example, with the company I wanted to take over, I had no intent of bringing about a wholesale loss of jobs. But the employees of that company feared they would be let go. Back then (B.S.), I had no sensitivity to that concern. The thought never crossed my mind! Now I really understand what it feels like to be afraid of losing a job. This country, this democracy, cannot function without benevolence. If we continue to lose the concept of benevolence, it's going to be an increasingly difficult struggle for everyone.

Today I see myself as a holder of a trust. I'm recognizing more and more that I have a God-given privilege and responsibility to demonstrate compassion. Those of us who have greater financial resources, also carry more responsibility to ease suffering in the world.

God has also taught me a lot in the last seven years about coping with stress. We live in a high-stress society, and I don't think that's ever going to change. I'm learning how to deal with stress in manageable ways.

"Avoid Unnecessary Stress"

First, I make a conscious effort to avoid unnecessary stress. I now give myself more than enough time to get to places without having to rush against the clock. For example, for the most part I've eliminated traffic-jam stress. When the stoplight turns red, I simply stop and wait for it to turn green—patiently and stress-free! Or, if the expressway is backed up, no problem. No matter how hard I try, I can't control or hurry up stoplights or rush-hour traffic; but I can take charge of the amount of time I've allowed to get to where I'm going. As much as possible, I work around situations involving time restraints. With minimal planning, and perhaps a little creativity, it's not that difficult to do. However, this does not come naturally to me, and I have to work at it.

A second area I'm learning about that also goes counter to my nature: I'm "growing" my confidence in the absolute sovereignty of God. Scripture is very clear that *God is in control*—whether I think He is or not! My opinion in this matter is irrelevant. I regularly and repeatedly choose to believe that. I've highlighted key passages of Scripture in my Bible to remind myself continually of this nonnegotiable truth—though honestly, especially in certain situations, my emotions don't always line up with my belief. Even so, by the choice of my will, I believe in faith (and declare it to myself often) that God *is* in control!

A third technique for coping with stress that works for me is to focus on the task at hand. This is more in line with who I am. I tend to be a single-minded person. But, when a lot of things are going on all at once, it's still a challenge for me to pull it off. I consciously determine to give myself fully to today's agenda, do the best job I can, then move on, and not worry about it. I try not to crucify myself on the cross of yesterday's regrets or on the cross of tomorrow's potentialities.

Finally, the fourth area that's been a major stress-reliever for me is to accept people for who they are. I'm learning to look at people through the window of their strengths rather than through the gridwork of my mind. Every individual is unique for whom Christ has died. It's not *my* job to "fix" anyone. It's my responsibility to be gracious and caring. I still try to be hard on problems, but easy on people. I can't imagine that I'll ever be a warm, fuzzy, "win friends and influence people" type person; but the realization that people are more important than principles and procedures has taken a lot of relational stress out of my life. I have definitely learned the value and significance of having caring friends.

❀ ❀ ❀

Work As Stress

"Three-quarters of the American public (76 percent) admit to living with a notable amount of stress, while 26 percent say they have 'a lot of stress' in their lives," according to the Mitchum Report on stress in the nineties, conducted by Research and Forecasts, Inc., a public opinion and market research firm. "One in three Americans cite work as the single most common source of stress. And 50 percent say their lives are more stressful now than five years ago."

A national survey by Northwestern National Life Insurance Company discovered that "seven out of ten employed Americans often experience stress-related conditions, such as exhaustion, anger or anxiety, muscle pain, headaches, inability to sleep, respiratory illness, ulcers or intestinal disorders, depression and hypertension."

The president of the American Institute of Stress, a non-profit educational clearinghouse for information on stress in Yonkers, New York, Dr. Paul J. Rosch, reports "more than 66 percent of all visits to primary-care physicians are for stress-related complaints."

Recent studies and current statistics only reinforce Daryle Doden's comment: "We live in a high-stress society, and I don't think that's ever going to change." If anything, reasons for stress in North American culture are on the rise. Society is increasingly complex. And life's pace has consistently sped up over the past two decades. With car phones, beepers, fax machines, and computer technology that produces almost instant results, it seems that there's no getting away from the demands and pressures of life.

Stress-management is becoming big business. Michael Castleman reports in *Men's Health* (July–August '91) on some of the coping techniques the experts not only suggest, but also practice themselves. Here are some excerpts:

> **Dr. Meyer Friedman, director of the Meyer Friedman Institute at Mt. Zion Medical Center in San Francisco, has developed what he calls the "five-year test." He says, "When a commitment looms—a concert, a dinner out, a conference—I ask myself, 'Will I care about this five years from now?' If so, I accept. If not, I decline. The five-year test puts things into perspective. You'd be amazed how trivial most engagements are. Once I started refusing invitations, I had more time for the things I considered *really* important: my family, my friends and my work."

> **Amy L. Flowers, a psychologist at Focal Pointe Women in Macon, Georgia, has personally determined to "lend a hand." She says, "Every Friday for 90 minutes at lunch I become the Beverage Lady at a local soup kitchen. I serve coffee, tea, and juice to people whose problems are much bigger than mine—poverty, home-

lessness, paralyzing disabilities. Having direct contact with folks with *real* problems is a big stress-reliever."

**Dr. Paul J. Rosch, already quoted above, says, "Events themselves aren't stressful—it's how we *perceive* them that makes us feel tense. For some a roller-coaster ride is distressing; for others, it's a pleasurable thrill. In general, stress comes from feeling out of control.... The real key to relieving stress is gaining control over irritants you have the power to change and *accepting* those you don't. There's a lot of truth to the prayer..., 'God grant me the courage to change what I can, the strength to accept what I can't, and the wisdom to know the difference.' "

**Allen Elkin, director of the Stress Management and Counseling Center in New York City, reports, "When I'm late for an appointment, or I'm having trouble getting the kids dressed for school and out the door, life's just a hassle. But if I 'awfulize' the situation by turning it into a personal catastrophe, I tense with stress. So, I rate the problem on a scale of one to ten, with ten being the worst—death of a loved one or loss of a job. Getting the kids dressed rates about a one. Spilling coffee on my tie is a two. If I rate my reaction to either situation, say, a seven, I know I'm overreacting."

Myriad of Coping Techniques

In light of what the stress-management gurus are saying and doing, Daryle Doden's right on target. The fact is, there are a myriad of coping techniques available to all of us. Physical exercise, soothing music, meditation, deep breathing, weekend getaways, sporting activities, support groups, hot baths, jet tubs, saunas, facials, personal alone moments, unplugging the telephone, getting "lost" in a good book, set times with close friends, hobbies... and on and on the possibilities go. The options are almost endless. And it's critically important in these changing times for each of us to deal proactively with our stress levels and learn the techniques that work best for us. It's a necessary survival skill for the nineties and beyond. Reality is, however, Christians have a decided advantage regarding off-loading stress. And too often we overlook the obvious.

Believers are assured and instructed in Psalm 46, "God is our refuge and strength, an ever present help in trouble. Therefore we will not fear . . . The Lord Almighty is with us . . . Be still, and know that I am God . . . The Lord Almighty is . . . our fortress" (vv. 1-2, 7-11).

Unfortunately—as was the case with Daryle Doden—some believers have unwittingly allowed knowing *about* God theologically to become a substitute for a close personal relationship *with* Him. To be a spiritual survivor, however, an essential part of the equation—especially when life is frenzied and full of stress—is carving out regular time to build a meaningful, intimate relationship *with* Jesus Christ. Just knowing the facts of Scripture will not suffice. What's most crucial is pursuing a growing personal relationship with the God of Scripture!

Peter, a devoted follower of Jesus, tells us, "Cast all your anxiety on Him because He cares for you . . . standing firm in the faith, because you know that your brothers throughout the world are undergoing the same kind of sufferings. And the God of all grace . . . after you have suffered a little while, will Himself restore you and make you strong, firm and steadfast" (1 Peter 5:7, 9-10, NIV).

In Philippians 4:6, the Apostle Paul encourages us (and he's serious!) "Do not be anxious about anything . . . [instead] . . . present your requests [your concerns, your stress —you name it] to God."

The words are comforting. It all sounds great. But exactly how do we pull this off . . . really?

Well, Valerie and I (along with thousands of others) are learning the powerful technique of off-loading stress through a simple prayer discipline. It's a practical prayer approach that was created through a team effort at The Chapel of the Air Ministries. And it works! The prayer can be readily adapted to fit any circumstances.

There's nothing supernatural about the precise words, but

there is real comfort in being reminded that the Almighty God cares about every detail of our lives. We encourage you to pray it regularly—preferably daily, or even several times a day.

Join Daryle Doden, Valerie Bell, me, and thousands of others who are learning to look to God for help in managing our stress. We offer this prayer to you as an achievable way to allow God to recalibrate your life according to His purposes for you.

Off-Loading Stress Prayer

Father,

You are God, even in stress-filled times.

On my own I could feel overwhelmed,

But Scripture tells me You care about every detail of my life.

Right now, the stress I feel most intensely is:

(fill in blank)
____

Show me the steps I can take, and give me the courage to take them.

Calm my spirit, Lord, as I trust You to bring good in this situation.

Amen.

CHAPTER EIGHT

TRAITS OF SPIRITUAL SURVIVORS

Steve and Valerie Bell

We are hard pressed on every side, but not crushed; perplexed, but not in despair; persecuted, but not abandoned; struck down, but not destroyed. . . . Therefore we do not lose heart. Though outwardly we are wasting away, yet inwardly we are being renewed day by day. For our light and momentary troubles are achieving for us an eternal glory that far outweighs them all. So we fix our eyes not on what is seen, but on what is unseen. For what is seen is temporary, but what is unseen is eternal.

2 Corinthians 4:8-9, 16-18

We come into this world with our fingers curled and only slowly, by repeated practice, do we learn to open our hands. It takes a great deal of dying to get us ready to live.

Virginia Stem Owens
Wind River Winter

Our phone rang as we were working on this final chapter. It was an old childhood friend. "We just wanted to let you know that Dad passed away yesterday. It was unexpected—so it came as a shock to all of us! Since he wasn't much of a churchgoer in his last few years, we're just having a short service for him at the funeral home. Come if you can."

We attended this good man's memorial service. It was standing room only. He knew a lot of people. During the service his friends and children spoke well of him. They eulogized his devotion to his family and his concern for others. They laughed about his wonderful sense of humor. He was obviously deeply loved, and everyone would miss him.

But it seemed odd to us that this man—who had sent his children to Christian grade school, high school, and college, who had made most of his lifetime friendships in the church, and who had lived such a moral life—had not one word mentioned during his farewell service about God or the hope of the believer for eternal life.

Something was missing!

It became sadly obvious. This good, loving, delightful, family man, who had started with God, did not manage to end with God. We have no idea what the turning point was. Perhaps his faith simply atrophied with disillusionment, disinterest, or disuse. But how tragic that a man who had apparently lived well for most of his life, did not end well!

Becoming a spiritual survivor is not easy. It doesn't happen automatically just because someone's a Christian. Spiritual survival is an acquired skill—it has to be learned.

Jesus, however, has clearly promised His devoted followers that the Father "will give you another Counselor to be with you forever—the Spirit of Truth . . . for He lives with you and will be in you. I will not leave you as orphans; I will come to you" (John 14:16-18). The point being, we who are believers can take confidence because the Bible states explicitly that we will never be left on our own.

In fact, the writer of Hebrews assures us that Jesus, the Son of God, is able to sympathize with us in every way—no matter what we may experience. Consequently, we are urged, "Let us then approach the throne of grace with confidence, so that we may receive mercy and find grace to help us in our time of need" (Heb. 4:16).

In light of these biblical truths, the questions raised in chapter 1 must be addressed.

Why is it that one person, who experiences despairing circumstances, is able to survive spiritually, and yet another, facing similar problems (maybe not even as intense), becomes a spiritual casualty? What is it that makes the difference?

Why are some believers able to face the worst life can throw at them, and their faith stays intact—actually deepens—while others seem to fade and fall away?

Why is it that two people can lean over the abyss of faithlessness—one will come back to God, but the other plunges over the edge?

Are there some special secrets to spiritual survival? If so, what are they?

We want to make seven observations that seem to characterize spiritual survivors. This is not a rigid formula for spiritual fidelity, but rather, some observations about common traits or "secrets" that mark the personal lives of those who stay with God.

These observations come out of the lives of Marshall and Susan Shelley, Ed Sansovini, Jim and Cindy Judge, Pamela Wexler-Smith, Bill and Edith Rediger, and Daryle Doden. We're indebted to each of them for their openness, honesty, and willingness to share their personal journeys with us.

Observation #1: *Spiritual survivors resolve their feelings about God.*

Crisis seems to be the real test of our theology. It forces our faith out of the academic and into life. Until we bump up against an extreme trial, we may not know what kind of faith we actually have.

In a sense, crisis reveals our most vulnerable area, where our faith may be weakest. For example, Ed Sansovini experienced a test of his affections . . . where was his heart? He came face to face with a jealous God and then wondered whether he could ever be forgiven. Pamela Wexler-Smith had a father-hunger. Following the death of her husband, her own battle with cancer (leukemia) was the crisis that brought her lifelong need for an understanding, dependable father to the forefront. Would God, her Heavenly Father, prove as unreliable as her earthly father? Or could she trust her Heavenly Father to "be there" for her? Daryle Doden questioned whether the God he had spent a lifetime learning about in the general sense, would exist for him in the real sense. Could he count on God being personally involved in his life when he had related to Him primarily as a principle-giver and enforcer of rules? Would God's everlasting arms catch him before his life was shattered?

Our soul's deepest need is exposed in crisis.

In each of the stories included in this book, we hear an echo of Jesus' plea; "My God, My God, why have You forsaken Me?" The variations of this question, asked by all of the spiritual survivors in the preceding chapters, are indicative of their emotional honesty. None of them held back. It's as though they went for God's jugular, contending with Him for some answers: "God, do You really care about me? Why are You so silent? Are You hurting with me, or are You just up there laughing? Why don't You take care of this right now? Are You punishing me? How long will this go on? Have You abandoned me? Why don't You intervene? How could You let this happen?"

Questions like these reveal a wide range of intense emotions directed toward God—doubt, fear, frustration, anger. We've heard these kinds of questions before—in the Bible! Job, not a man of weak faith, asked similar questions, and God felt these very human responses were important enough to include in the scriptural account.

What differentiates the faithful from those who fall away is that spiritual survivors eventually move beyond this stage of rage or disillusionment with God. In time, they resolve their feelings about God. All of the survivors you've met in this book came to a point of decision. In one way or another each one was finally able to say, "I don't understand what's happening. It doesn't make any sense to me, but I will trust God because I believe He is *for* me."

Even while life is unraveling, spiritual survivors choose to believe God is still in control. In *Disappointment with God,* Philip Yancey wrote of this mind-set: "Saints become saints by somehow hanging on to the stubborn conviction that things are not as they appear, and that the unseen world is as solid and trustworthy as the visible world around them. God deserves trust, even when it looks like the world is caving in. 'The world was not worthy of them,' Hebrews 11 concludes about its amazing assemblage, adding this intriguing comment: 'Therefore God is not ashamed to be called their God.' "

In the process of clarifying their feelings about God, spiritual survivors also determine who their real enemy is. They recognize that Satan is the author of evil, not God. And though evil abounds, they trust God to ultimately prevail.

Spiritual survivors often report a renewed love and intimacy with God. Pamela Wexler-Smith, because of her suffering, arrived at the point where she could call God "the Father of Extreme Understanding." Spiritual survivors grasp the crux of Christianity as expressed by Frederick Buechner: "To be commanded to love God at all, let alone in the wilderness, is like being commanded to be well when we are sick, to sing for joy when we are dying of thirst, to run when our legs are broken. But this is the first and great commandment nonetheless. Even in the wilderness—especially in the wilderness—you shall love Him."

Observation #2: *Spiritual survivors find courage in the example of other sufferers.*

When it comes to crisis, it's typical to think that our own situation is the worst. At least it usually feels that way. But spiritual survivors learn to lift their eyes beyond themselves to gain perspective on their suffering.

For example, it's Bill Rediger saying, though their precious teenage daughter was murdered, about that same time, they had heard of another family who had tragically lost five children at once. It's Pamela Wexler-Smith who realized that, although she was a young widow who closely resembled a holocaust victim, many of those who started chemotherapy with her did not even survive the treatment. At least she was alive! It's Daryle Doden reading about Pastor Don Baker's more severe depression and concluding, if Pastor Baker could get better, so could he.

Though most of us are apt to think "our situation is the worst," it's important to understand that all over the world the righteous are suffering. Jesus Himself said it rains on the just and the unjust (Matt. 5:45). To experience life is to know some heartbreak. That's the reality factor—no one is exempt!

If we want to be among those who stay with God, and if we want to triumph over whatever difficult situations may come along, then it will be necessary for us to keep our suffering in perspective. Look around regularly. Intense suffering surrounds us. Some people's situations are horrific, yet they go on with their lives. We can too.

Observation #3: *Spiritual survivors draw strength from the community of believers, the church.*
God designed us to experience faith in community. And what better place is there than the church when it comes to providing comfort, care, understanding, love, and needed encouragement? When the church gets it right, it really gets it right!

We love the different "snapshots" of God's church at work that we've seen through the real-life stories of our spiritual survivors. There's Ed Sansovini going to the prison post office and finding a huge bag of mail, bursting with over 700 cards and letters from the people of his church, all saying in a variety of ways, "We love you." Or envision Marshall and Susan Shelley trying to locate Mandy—the church baby—at the end of an evening gathering only to find that she had been passed from one loving set of arms to another. Or think of Bill and Edith Rediger whose church friends persisted in spending time with them during those initial weeks following Cindy's disappearance, and caring enough to keep their refrigerator overflowing with food—more than they could ever eat! Picture a congregation, led by their pastor, searching the church campus on a dark Sunday night for a despondent and desperate young businessman and father, Daryle Doden; then finding him not far from the pond—and rescuing him from himself.

In *Mere Christianity,* C.S. Lewis wrote of the interaction of believers within Christ's body: "God can show Himself as He really is only to real men. And that means not simply to men who are individually good, but to men who are united together in a body, loving one another, helping one another, showing Him to one another. For that is what God meant humanity to be like; like players in one band, or organs in one body."

When life's overwhelming circumstances engulf them, spiritual survivors eventually acknowledge they need help. They learn that times of crisis are not times to practice spiritual individualism. Instead, they allow the community of believers to minister to them. They take their comfort from those who not only share a pew, but share a commitment to one another as well.

Observation #4: *Spiritual survivors take comfort as the Scriptures come alive.*

It's almost uncanny how often God ministers to the specific needs of individuals through His Word. But then . . . God is supernatural! In 2 Timothy 3:16, we're told, "All Scripture is God-breathed and is useful for teaching, rebuking, correcting and training." So should we really be all that surprised? Even so, spiritual survivors repeatedly verify this supernatural phenomenon. It's as though certain parts of Scripture jump out at them addressing their particular situation. Though the passage may have been read before—perhaps the verses are even familiar ones—the spiritual impact is so potent it's as if they are seeing the significance of these truths for the first time. Marshall Shelley stated it— ". . . different parts of Scripture really came alive to me . . . and . . . stood out in technicolor!"

While in prison Ed Sansovini found tremendous comfort in the Psalms—especially Psalms 50 and 51, which he said he must have read through hundreds of times. "Even though I had studied Scripture for years . . . old texts just sort of popped up from nowhere and really ministered to me . . . like the verse, 'My time is in Thy hands.' "

Pamela Wexler-Smith even expressed a desire to be ministered to by other believers through God's own words. "One of the most helpful spiritual exercises to me is when we who are believers speak God's Word to one another rather than just expressing our own sense of sympathy or empathy about another person's problem."

Through the centuries spiritual survivors have testified that in times of darkness and despair, God's Word "is a lamp to my feet and a light for my path" (Ps. 119:105).

While trying to get through seemingly impossible situations, spiritual survivors remain open to a special touch from God. And frequently that touch of the supernatural comes through Scripture as the Holy Spirit empowers a passage to minister effectively in a given situation.

Observation #5: *Spiritual survivors focus on today.* Survivors, those who remain faithful to God, realize they have only to get through one day at a time. Like Daryle Doden said, "I consciously determine to give myself fully to today's agenda . . . I try not to crucify myself on the cross of yesterday's regrets, or . . . tomorrow's potentialities."

Each of us probably knows someone with a past so miserable that he or she is drowning in self-pity. To be a spiritual survivor requires letting go of the injustices suffered, the pain others have caused us, the disappointments we've experienced, and getting on with the job of living in the now.

"Not one of us can bring back yesterday or shape tomorrow," says Frederick Buechner in *The Hungering Dark.* He adds, "Only today is ours and it will not be ours for long; and once it is gone, it will never in all time be ours again."

Though the future is uncertain, we have today. Living in the present means learning to appreciate the beauty of the moment—whether it's noticing a waddling mother duck and her downy ducklings like Ed Sansovini did within the confines of prison, or enjoying an outing with your children listening to the "oldie goldie" station and laughing until your sides ache like Pamela Wexler-Smith did even though the possibility of a recurrence of leukemia still loomed.

Living today to the full is also Dr. Jim Judge working all day long in a mission hospital dealing with AIDS patients and other life-and-death situations, but then spending that evening playing board games with his children and having a meaningful conversation with his wife.

When involved in difficult, stressful situations, a key survival skill is giving yourself permission to enjoy what's positive—the little things—whether they're crisp clean sheets on your bed, or a delicious seven-layer salad, or friends who make you get out and play tennis, or children who brighten the room when they walk in, or a beautiful sunset—or any delightful happening that we typically take for granted. Making this a habit might be just what's needed to get through any given day.

Observation #6: *Spiritual survivors acknowledge personal growth through their suffering.*

"Human beings grow by striving, working, stretching; and in a sense, human nature needs problems more than solutions," writes Philip Yancey in *Disappointment with God.* He adds, "Paradoxically, the most perplexing, Job-like times may help 'fertilize' faith and nurture intimacy with God. The deepest faith . . . sprouts at a point of contradiction, like a blade of grass between stones."

If you could sit for a while, as we have, and have a personal conversation with each of the spiritual survivors included in this book, every one of them would attest to specific areas of spiritual growth or maturity that have come about because of the situations they've encountered. Jim and Cindy Judge, after coming back from a year of short-term missionary service in Africa, have managed to maintain a downscaled lifestyle. Both of them say they continue to have a deeper sense of intimacy and peace in their personal walks with the Lord. They are mutually committed to living with less stress and fostering a kingdom mind-set. They're still learning about establishing limits and setting personal boundaries so they can remain available to "risk" with God!

Pamela Wexler-Smith reports that her perspective about life has radically changed. "I have refocused my life on what is real and lasting . . . I notice others' pain, and I hurt with them . . . the trites and trivias of this life are now treated as such. In many respects I feel that this suffering experience has helped me rise above life's garbage. . . ."

Bill Rediger talks about how the suffering they've experienced has taught him to be more thankful for what he does have—his two daughters, the grandchildren, his marriage, good health, their friends, the church. "There are so many good things in our lives, and they've all come into focus more clearly because of the pain and suffering we've experienced as a family."

Daryle Doden speaks of a new sensitivity, a new compassion for others growing out of his journey into despair and depression. "Probably more than anything else . . . I now believe that people are more important than principles and procedures . . . My relationship with God and with others must be primary and foremost." His experience has even changed his attitude about how he approaches making business decisions.

Though, in every case, personal and spiritual growth has been produced, we know that those, who have gone through intense struggle and suffering to get to where they are, would never choose to relive their pain. Even so, it's common for spiritual survivors to talk about significant lessons learned from their experiences.

Observation #7: *Spiritual survivors tolerate life's unanswered questions.*

Kierkegaard compared Christians to schoolboys who want to turn to the back of their books to find the answers to their math problems rather than working through them.

That's true! Life can feel like an exercise in problem-solving without guarantees that there will be solutions in the back of the book or any place else. Living without the answers to a difficult life problem can produce enormous tension. And yet, that is exactly what many spiritual survivors live with every day—lingering unanswered questions.

We liked how Marshall Shelley expressed it in passing during one of our conversations: "Someday, I'm going to get in that long heavenly line of believers who are there to have their questions answered."

There is a definite longing for the day when God will make sense of our suffering. But, in the meantime, survivors live with loose ends, uncertainty, and situations that defy all reason.

Spiritual survivors seem to hold to a future hope, a belief, that God will pronounce meaning on all the chapters of their lives—and that from some of the apparently tragic chapters, eternal good will prevail.

We love the fable Max Lucado shares in *In the Eye of the Storm:*

> Once there was an old man who lived in a tiny village. Although poor, he was envied by all, for he owned a beautiful white horse. Even the king coveted his treasure. A horse like this had never been seen before—such was its splendor, its majesty, its strength.
>
> People offered fabulous prices for the steed, but the old man always refused. "This horse is not a horse to me," he would tell them. "It is a person. How could you sell a person? He is a friend, not a possession. How could you sell a friend?" The man was poor and the temptation was great. But he never sold the horse.
>
> One morning he found that the horse was not in the stable. All the village came to see him. "You old fool," they scoffed, "we told you that someone would steal your horse. We warned you that you would be robbed. You are so poor. How could you ever hope to protect such a valuable animal? It would have been better to have sold him. You could have gotten whatever price you wanted. No amount would have been too high. Now the horse is gone, and you've been cursed with misfortune."
>
> The old man responded, "Don't speak too quickly. Say only that the horse is not in the stable. That is all we know; the rest is judgment. If I've been cursed or not, how can you know? How can you judge?"
>
> The people contested, "Don't make us out to be fools!

We may not be philosophers, but great philosophy is not needed. The simple fact that your horse is gone is a curse."

The old man spoke again. "All I know is that the stable is empty, and the horse is gone. The rest I don't know. Whether it be a curse or a blessing, I can't say. All we can see is a fragment. Who can say what will come next?"

The people of the village laughed. They thought that the man was crazy. They had always thought he was a fool; if he wasn't, he would have sold the horse and lived off the money. But instead, he was a poor woodcutter, an old man still cutting firewood and dragging it out of the forest and selling it. He lived hand to mouth in the misery of poverty. Now he had proven that he was, indeed, a fool.

After fifteen days, the horse returned. He hadn't been stolen; he had run away into the forest. Not only had he returned, he had brought a dozen wild horses with him. Once again the village people gathered around the woodcutter and spoke. "Old man, you were right and we were wrong. What we thought was a curse was a blessing. Please forgive us."

The man responded, "Once again, you go too far. Say only that the horse is back. State only that a dozen horses returned with him, but don't judge. How do you know if this is a blessing or not? You see only a fragment. Unless you know the whole story, how can you judge? You read only one page of a book. Can you judge the whole book? You read only one word of a phrase. Can you understand the entire phrase?

"Life is so vast, yet you judge all of life with one page or one word. All you have is a fragment! Don't say that this is a blessing. No one knows. I am content with what I know. I am not perturbed by what I don't."

"Maybe the old man is right," they said to one another. So they said little. But down deep, they knew he was wrong. They knew it was a blessing. Twelve wild horses had returned with one horse. With a little bit of work, the animals could be broken and trained and sold for much money.

The old man had a son, an only son. The young man began to break the wild horses. After a few days, he fell from one of the horses and broke both legs. Once again the villagers gathered around the old man and cast their judgments.

"You were right," they said. "You proved you were right. The dozen horses were not a blessing. They were a curse. Your son has broken his legs, and now in your old age you have no one to help you. Now you are poorer than ever."

The old man spoke again. "You people are obsessed with judging. Don't go so far. Say only that my son broke his legs. Who knows if it is a blessing or a curse? No one knows. We only have a fragment. Life comes in fragments."

It so happened that a few weeks later the country engaged in war against a neighboring country. All the young men of the village were required to join the army. Only the son of the old man was excluded, because he was injured. Once again the people gathered around the old man, crying and screaming because their sons had been taken. There was little chance they would return. The enemy was strong, and the war would be a losing struggle. They would never see their sons again.

"You were right, old man," they wept. "God knows you were right. This proves it. Your son's accident was a blessing. His legs may be broken, but at least he is with you. Our sons are gone forever."

The old man spoke again. "It is impossible to talk with you. You always draw conclusions. No one knows. Say only this: Your sons had to go to war, and mine did not. No one knows if it is a blessing or a curse. No one is wise enough to know. Only God knows."

And that's how life is. Things are not always what they appear to be. For the present time, we can only look at fragments of information as situations unfold. But we anticipate a time when God will write the final eternal chapter, and we will see the entire picture of our lives and understand the meaning of all our experiences.

Spiritual survivors trust God to write those final chapters well. And because they look at life with a perspective broader than the present, they maintain a sense of hope.

The challenge facing each of us who has started with God is to stay with God! That means maintaining a kingdom mindset and living our ordinary days to the full, persevering with God through whatever crises come along, and then finally, being found faithful in that moment when we take our last earthly breath and surrender our lives eternally to God.

May these words be true for those who want to finish well:

O Jesus, I have promised
To serve Thee to the end;
Be Thou forever near me,
My Master and my Friend:
I shall not fear the battle
If Thou art by my side,
Nor wander from the pathway
If Thou wilt be my guide.

O let me feel Thee near me;
The world is ever near;
I see the sights that dazzle,
The tempting sounds I hear:
My foes are ever near me,
Around me and within;
But Jesus, draw Thou nearer,
And shield my soul from sin.

O Jesus, Thou hast promised
To all who follow Thee,
That where Thou art in glory,
There shall Thy servant be;
And, Jesus, I have promised
To serve Thee to the end;
O give me grace to follow,
My Master and my Friend.

John E. Bode